BLACK-WHITE RACIAL ATTITUDES

AN ANNOTATED BIBLIOGRAPHY

Constance E. Obudho

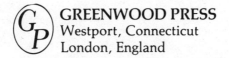

GREENWOOD PRESS
Westport, Connecticut
London, England

To my mother
Barbara P. Beckwith

Library of Congress Cataloging in Publication Data

Obudho, Constance E
  Black-white racial attitudes.

  Includes indexes.
  1. United States—Race question—Bibliography.
  2. Attitude (Psychology)—Bibliography. 3. Negroes—Race
  identity—Bibliography. I. Title.
  Z1361.N39028 1976   [E185.61]   016.30145′1′0420973
  ISBN 0-8371-8582-3   75-35351

Library of Congress Catalog Card Number: 75-35351
ISBN: 0-8371-8582-3

First published in 1976

Greenwood Press, a division of Williamhouse-Regency Inc.
51 Riverside Avenue, Westport, Connecticut 06880

Printed in the United States of America

CONTENTS

PREFACE

This bibliography presents annotations of articles and books concerned with various aspects of the racial attitudes of blacks and whites in the United States. The works cited contain information about the racial attitudes of blacks and whites toward each other and toward their own group, some of the factors associated with racial attitudes, and attitude formation and change in children and adults.

The works included in the bibliography cover the period from 1950 to 1974. Books and articles appearing under the individual headings are in alphabetical order by author. Each author's name is preceded by an entry number, and these run consecutively from the first to the last section. In addition, each annotation is a description of the work and does not include a critique of the material. Each source has been categorized according to its greatest relevance to a section. When a work appeared to be related to more than one section, it was put in what was felt to be the most appropriate category. If the particular journal or book was not available or when pages were missing from a journal, the annotations have been summarized directly from the *Psychological Abstracts*, in which the works were indexed.

The bibliography is divided into the following sections: Racial Attitude Formation and Change in Children, Racial Attitudes in Young People, Racial Attitude Change in Adults, Concomitants of Racial Attitudes, and Racial Attitudes in Adults.

I hope that this book will serve as a convenient reference tool for those people interested in race relations. However, any bibliography is subject to omissions and errors; I would appreciate hearing from readers who can supply additions or corrections.

I would like to express my gratitude to my husband who helped me organize the bibliography and who patiently looked after our children while I wrote. I would also like to express my appreciation to Mrs. Cecilia Harberster who did a wonderful job in typing the manuscript.

INTRODUCTION

RACE RELATIONS: A HISTORICAL PERSPECTIVE

A variety of beliefs, attitudes, and actions are described by the term "race relations." The state of the relationship between blacks and whites in the United States is often a source of concern to interested citizens because of its somewhat precarious nature. Consequently, many social scientists and others have been sensitive to the importance of attempting to describe and understand various aspects of this phenomenon.

Reuter (1970, pp. 84-95) traced the present condition of the relationship between blacks and whites in America back to earlier conditions that developed from the introduction of black Africans as slaves into the society. The slave system and social attitudes and racial doctrines formulated by whites in reaction to this system contributed to the resulting relationship.

Strong (1965, p. 34) asserted that the beginning of racial conflict in America could not be given a specific date. He suggested instead that there were four outstanding periods in the history of race relations which could be marked with dates of court decisions.

The first period was in 1661, when for the first time, the law permitted life enslavement. This event marked the end of indentured service for whites and the beginning of life enslavement for blacks in this country. The second period was reflected in the famous *Scott* v. *Sanford* decision, in which the Supreme Court ruled that a black person whose ancestors were slaves was not entitled to the rights of an American citizen and, therefore, had no standing in court. A third period was heralded by the *Plessy* v. *Ferguson* case (1896), which established the "separate but equal" doctrine. The final landmark came in 1954 with the *Brown* v. *Board of Education* decision, which effectively overruled the separate but equal doctrine and declared that segregation in public schools based on race or color was unconstitutional.

Certain social philosophies also have shaped the development of race-related attitudes. According to *Institutional Racism in America* (1969, pp. 9-14) "social Darwinism," "manifest destiny," and "the white man's burden" affected race relations. Darwin's theory of the survival of the fittest was used by many whites to support their claim that the poverty and degradation of blacks were the result of an innate lack of ability. According to the idea of manifest destiny, territorial expansion and domination by the white race was inevitable in the history of America. Finally, the white man's burden was a responsibility to Christianize and civilize the inferior darker races.

Thus it can be seen that a number of forces contributed to establishing a social order that recognized black people as inferior. In the view of the dominant white race, good race relations hinged on the willingness of black people to accept a subordinant role, or, "to keep their place." Understandably, black people could not embrace this view.

The twentieth century has seen many changes in the relations between the races. Brown (1973, p. 4) sees as especially significant the recent shift in focus from integration to black separatism, from nonviolent marches and sit-ins to militancy in action and rhetoric, and the acceptance of some mililtant blacks of the use of any means to gain desired ends.

The friction between blacks and whites tended toward open conflict in the 1950s and 1960s, as Keesing's Research Report noted (1970, p. 1). The slow progress of civil rights legislation in the mid-1960s contributed to the friction and engendered an increasingly militant mood among blacks in the nation. The number of race riots in this decade led President Lyndon B. Johnson to establish a Special Advisory Commission on Civil Disorders in 1967.

Unfortunately, the state of the relationship between blacks and whites in America remains precarious in the seventies. School segregation, discrimination in housing, discrimination in jobs, and discrimination in social facilities, for example, are still outstanding problems. As Reuter (1970, p. 96) asserted, the racial sentiment and attitudes that were defined in the slave relationship are still operative today. The long-standing conception by whites of their superiority over blacks is so completely a part of a way of thinking that there is an unwillingness to consider change and an inability to understand the possibility of other types of racial relationships. It is to be hoped that this view is too negative, and in the not too distant future more favorable conditions will exist.

TERMINOLOGY FOR RACIAL ATTITUDES

In many of the works presented in this bibliography, the concepts prejudice, stereotyping, ethnocentrism, attitudes, or preferences were used to describe the race-related behavior exhibited by individuals toward those of another race or toward members of their own race. These terms are sometimes used interchangeably and depend upon the particular preference of the experimenter or writer. However, since some of these concepts have distinct meanings, it would be appropriate to discuss them briefly.

In his book *The Nature of Prejudice* (1958), Gordon W. Allport defined ethnic prejudice as "an antipathy based upon a faulty and inflexible generalization. It may be felt or expressed. It may be directed toward a group as a whole, or toward an individual because he is a member of that group [p. 10]." Allport defined the term stereotype as "an exaggerated belief (favorable or unfavorable) associated with a category. Its function is to justify (rationalize) our conduct in relation to that category [p. 187]."

The term ethnocentrism was first introduced and used in 1906 by Summer. D. J. Levinson (1949) defines it as a provincialism or cultural narrowness that results in a tendency in the individual to be rigid in his acceptance of the unlike (p. 19). The term is further defined as "an ideology: a relatively stable system of opinions, attitudes, and values [p. 19]." Levinson defines attitudes as an individual's readiness for action. They include all of the person's ideas about what should be done to, for, or against any social entity.

And lastly, the term preference is usually used to refer to an individual's choice of one racial group over another because of favorable feelings toward the former group.

THE FORMATION OF RACIAL ATTITUDES

All individuals develop particular ways of thinking, believing, and acting toward the various racial groups within their society. Once formed, the patterns of thought and behavior are often difficult to change. Nevertheless, an important question is, how are these thoughts and behaviors initially formed?

A number of factors are responsible for attitude formation. Among them are the primary group or family, the peer group, society in general, mass communication, and experiences.

Both Allport (1958) and S. C. Fisher (1948) believe that parents are usually the most influential forces in a child's life concerning which groups were acceptable or not acceptable and concerning the impartment of the moral codes of the society.

Regarding the peer group factor, A. Lichtenstein (1934) noted that children are exposed to the ideas of their friends who live in the neighborhood and those at school and that they acquire certain attitudes from them.

The society in which the individual grows and develops also influences the formation of his attitudes. Horowitz (1936) pointed out that the individual develops his attitudes and learns how he should respond toward various important objects in the society through cultural norms and traditional values taught by teachers, ministers, and others in addition to his family and friends who are important to him.

In addition to the attitudes developed through personal contact with a source of influence, W. W. Charters (1933) suggested that mass communication in the form of television, movies, newspapers, and books serves as a basis for many attitudes. Children and adults may be affected by what they view and read, and the media may help to formulate their opinions about others.

A final source of influence upon racial attitude formation may be personal experience. A. W. Foshay and K. D. Wann (1954) made the point that attitudes may be formed through the experience of some event or, in other words, through learning. An individual's personal contact with a member of a particular racial group may affect his racial attitudes.

Depending on an individual's personal contact with a member of a particular racial group may affect his racial attitudes.

Depending on an individual's stage in life, some of these factors may exert a stronger influence on attitude formation than others. However, all of these factors may influence an individual's attitudes toward various ethnic groups within his society.

REFERENCES

Allport, G. W. *The Nature of Prejudice*. Reading, Mass. Addison-Wesley Publishing Company, 1958.

Brown, I. C. *Understanding Race Relations*. Englewood Cliffs, N. J.: Prentice-Hall, 1973.

Charters, W. W. "Developing the Attitudes of Children." *Education*, 53, 1933, 353-357.

Fisher, S. C. *Relationships in Attitudes, Opinions, and Values Among Family Members*. University of California Publications in Culture and Society, 2(2), 1948.

Foshay, A. W. and Wann, K. D. *Children's Social Values*. New York: Teachers' College, Columbia University, 1954. 28-30.

Frazier, E. F. *On Race Relations: Selected Writings*. G. F. Edwards (Ed), Chicago: The University of Chicago Press, 1968.

Horowtiz, E. L. "The Development of Attitudes Toward the Negro." *Archives of Psychology*, No. 194, 1936, 34-35.

Institutional Racism in America. Louis L. Knowles and Kenneth Prewitt (Eds), Englewood Cliffs, N. J.: Prentice-Hall, 1969.

Keesing's Research Report. *Race Relations in the USA 1954-68* New York: Charles Scribner's Sons, 1970.

Levinson, D. J. "An Approach to the Theory and Measurement of Ethnocentric Ideology." *Journal of Psychology,* 1949, 1939.

Lichtenstein, A. *Can Attitudes Be Taught?* Baltimore, Md.: The Johns Hopkins Press, 1934.

Reuter, E. B. *The American Race Problem.* New York: Thomas Y. Crowell Company, 1970.

Strong, H. H. "Progress in Race Relations." *Journal of Human Relations,* 4(4), 1956, 34-42.

BLACK-WHITE RACIAL ATTITUDES

1

RACIAL ATTITUDE FORMATION AND CHANGE IN CHILDREN

1. Baker, E. A. and Owen, D. R. "Negro-white personality differences in integrated classrooms." Proceedings of the 77th Annual Convention of the American Psychological Association, 4(Pt. 2), 1969, 539-540.

Black males who had previously attended an all Black elementary school were compared with their new classmates during their first year in a predominantly White classroom. The students were contrasted on scales of the Missouri Children's Picture Series, a teacher's behavior checklist, IQ scores, and a socioeconomic status measure. Several of the measures were found to differentiate significantly in fall and spring testings. The nature of the measures is discussed and the most immediate behavioral implications are explored. (Summary of author abstract.)

2. Barber, R. W. "The effects of open enrollment on anti-Negro and anti-white prejudices among junior high school students in Rochester, New York." Dissertation Abstracts, 29(5-A), 1968, 1383-1384.

The purpose of the study was to examine whether limited desegregation in a predominantly White public school had an effect on students' anti-Black and anti-White prejudices. Eighth-grade students were subjects. Some of the findings were that there was a difference between the attitudes of Blacks and Whites toward each other in nonsegregated as opposed to segregated schools. In the integrated school, intense racial feelings were experienced. However, some interracial friendships were found to have developed.

3. Bienvenu, M. J. "Effects of school integration on the self-concept and anxiety of lower-class Negro adolescent males." Dissertation Abstracts, 29(2-A), 1968, 692.

The study was concerned with the effects of integration on lower-class Black male adolescents in terms of self-concept and level of manifest or overt anxiety. Some results were that a significant difference in self-concept was found between an experimental and a control

group in the postintegration situation. There was a
significant difference in the anxiety level of experimental group individuals from pre- to postintegration.
And high self-concept was usually correlated with lower
anxiety.

4. Campbell, E. Q. "Some socio-psychological correlates of
direction in attitude change." Social Forces, 36, 1958,
335-340.

The study reported tests of hypotheses regarding the
relationship of certain variables to the direction of
racial attitude change among high school students in a
southern community. The respondents were classified as
Nonchangers, Positive Changers, and Negative Changers
according to their before and after scores on the attitude measure. Campbell found that those who claimed
Blacks as personal friends on the After measure were more
likely to change scale positions in a positive direction
than those without Black friends. Those who had a large
number of classes with Blacks were not more likely to
show positive attitude change. And those who sense a
degree of attitude alienation from their significant
in-group changed in the direction of the perceived position of that in-group.

5. Campbell, J. D. and Yarrow, M. R. "Personal and situational variables in adaptation to change." Journal of Social
Issues, 14(1), 1958, 29-46.

Campbell and Yarrow discussed their investigation of the
effects of imposed desegregation on children's behavior
and attitudes. The discussion here was the final segment of three parts of a paper presented successively in
the same journal. Although many of the factors which
affected the process and outcome of induced change were
"afterthoughts" in the research design and were not
selected and varied on a systematic basis for study, it
was suggested that these findings may provoke more pene-
trating research questions concerning processes and
change in the individual as well as factors of change
in the natural setting.

6. Campbell, J. D., Yarrow, L. J., and Yarrow, M. R. "A
study of adaptation to a new situation." Journal of Social
Issues, 14(1), 1958, 3-7.

This is an introductory article which outlines a program
of research concerned with the adjustment of children to
a desegregated summer camp situation. Theory and data
from social psychological change studies and from child
development and socialization research contributed to
the formulation of the study.

7. Charley, B. H. "The effectiveness of Negro teachers for
changing developing racial attitudes in young children."

Dissertation Abstracts International, 131(2-A), 1970(Aug), 824.

Charley asserted that the equal status role specific hypothesis of attitude change in intergroup relations predicts that favorable attitude change by majority group members toward minority members occurs only toward minority individuals in roles in which the equal status contact occurred but would not be generalized to other role situations. Elementary school children who had either Black or White teachers were subjects. The results did not support the hypothesis. The students showed the characteristic pre-prejudicial preference pattern regardless of their teacher's race. It was suggested that cultural influences predispose children to prefer White people and are of such magnitude that contact in one role situation does not alter developing racial preference.

8. Crooks, R. C. "The effects of an interracial preschool program upon racial preference, knowledge of racial differences, and racial identification." Journal of Social Issues, 26(4), 1970, 137-144.

The study was a replication of the Clark and Clark 1939 investigation concerning awareness of racial differences, racial identification, and racial preference among young children. However, Crooks used both Black and White children, a White experimenter only, and determined the effect of a preschool program on the three responses. The results of Crooks' study supported the earlier ones by Clark and Clark and showed that (a) both races of children preferred the white dolls which served as stimuli for the racial measures; (b) only 24 percent of the Black children made correct racial identification choices, while 100 percent of the White children made the correct choice; and (c) Black children who experienced the preschool program showed greater own-race preference than did those who had not experienced it, and White children experiencing the program were more pro-Black than were Whites who had not been in the program.

9. Dimas, C. "The effect of motion pictures portraying black models on the self-concept of black elementary school children." Dissertation Abstracts International, 31(6-A), 1970(Dec), 2609-2610.

The purpose of the study was to determine whether there was a difference in the self-concept of Black students who saw motion pictures of Black models and those who saw motion pictures of White models. Black elementary school children were subjects. The results generally showed that students viewing the Black models indicated certain aspects of the self as being more positive than students who viewed the White models.

10. Epstein, R. and Komorita, S. S. "Childhood prejudice as
a function of parental ethnocentrism, punitiveness, and out-
group characteristics." Journal of Personality and Social
Psychology, 3(3), 1966, 259-264.

The major goal of the study was to investigate the development of social distance in children as a function of
perceived parental punitiveness toward aggression, perceived parental ethnocentrism, and two major outgroup
characteristics--social status and race. Boys and girls
in the third to fifth grades at a Catholic parochial
school were subjects. Each subject filled out the Parental Punitiveness Scale (PPS) developed by the authors
to measure children's perceptions of parental behavior
regarding this variable. The experimenters attempted to
"create specific cognitions regarding a fictitious group,
the Piraneans." Subjects were shown slides of middle-
or lower-class Black, Oriental, or White male and female
children in groups of four (two of each sex) representing the subject's age range. After seeing the slides,
the subjects completed a social distance scale. Results
showed that the lower-class conditions elicited greater
social distance than middle class, and Blacks elicited
more social distance than Whites or Orientals. Additionally, the socioeconomic level X race interaction showed
that lower-status Blacks received greater social distance
responses than lower-status Whites and Orientals and
middle-class Blacks, Whites, and Orientals. It was also
found that social distance toward the fictitious group
was significantly correlated with the subject's general
level of ethnocentrism and with perceived parental prejudice toward the specific ethnic groups depicted on the
slides.

11. Golin, S. "Project self-esteem: Some effects of an
elementary school black studies program." Proceedings of
the Annual Convention of the American Psychological Association, 6(Pt. 2), 1971, 733-734.

The study reported some results of a project called
"Project Self-Esteem" which was designed to develop
Black consciousness in Black elementary school children.
The project involved school classes in Black art, music,
and dance; an after school program in art, music, and
dance; and a field program in which the students took
trips every month to businesses and exhibitions. The
program lasted through the fifth and sixth grades. The
results showed that participation in the project had a
positive effect on the mental health (self-esteem) particularly of the male children.

12. Hohn, R. L. "Perceptual training and its effect on
racial preferences of kindergarten children." Psychological
Reports, 32(2), 1973(Apr), 435-441.

The purpose of the study was to evaluate two training
procedures in facilitating racial preference in

kindergarten children. One treatment involved role-
taking ability and perceptual awareness and the other
involved training in conservation and spatial perspective. The subjects were given a racial preference test
in which they were asked to choose among pictures of
Black and White models. The findings showed that the
children preferred the White models. Both treatments
reduced pro-White biases. And, both treatments resulted
in the children acquiring conservation of number, distance, and two-dimensional space.

13. Holland, R. F. "The effects of two study units on high
school students' attitudes toward Negroes." Dissertation
Abstracts International, 30(5-A), 1969, 1775-1776.

The purpose of the study was to determine whether one of
two special study units was more effective than the other
in changing White eleventh- and twelfth-grade students'
attitudes toward Blacks. Both study units (one dealing
with attitudes toward Blacks and the other with attitudes
toward minorities in general) were effective in favorably
changing the attitudes of the students toward Blacks.

14. Katz, I., Hency, T., and Allen, H. "Effects of race of
tester, approval-disapproval, and need on Negro children's
learning." Journal of Personality and Social Psychology,
8(1, Pt. 1), 1968, 38-42.

Northern Black elementary school boys were given a
social desirability questionnaire and a verbal learning
task by Black and White male experimenters. Each subject received either approval or disapproval on the
learning task. It was found that performance was better
with Black testers and also when approval was given.
Additionally, the strength of the child's need for
approval influenced his reactions to the race of the
experimenter and approval.

15. Katz, P. A. "Stimulus predifferentiation and modification of children's racial attitudes." Child Development,
44(2), 1973(Jun), 232-237.

Katz tested the prediction that increased perceptual
differentiation of other-group faces would reduce prejudicial attitudes. Black and White elementary school
children who had previously scored high and low on social
attitude measures were subjects. They were assigned to
one of three training conditions: (1) learning distinctive names for pictures of other-race faces, (2)
making same-different judgments of facial pairs, or (3)
observing the faces without labels. The race of the
experimenter was varied within each group. The findings
supported the prediction. Posttest prejudice scores
were lower for the labeling and perceptual training
groups than for subjects not exposed to this training.
Furthermore, the results were influenced by level of
development and the race of the experimenter.

16. Kline, H. K. "An exploration of racism in ego ideal formation." Smith College Studies in Social Work, 40(3), 1970(Jun), 211-235.

The study examined a process through which social and psychological forces might converge in the formative years of life to institutionalize racism in the developing personality. Black and White kindergarten and first-grade children were subjects. Each child was individually interviewed concerning his ego ideal and was then presented, successively, with a doll of his own race and one of the other race. Each was asked to judge whether each doll would achieve his standard and which of the two would exceed this standard. The results were that most of the children in both racial groups predicted that both of the dolls would be successful in fulfilling a goal which they had presented. When asked which doll would more nearly attain the goal, White subjects more frequently chose the white doll. Although Black children favored the black doll, this judgment did not achieve statistical significance. Lastly, White children predicted the success of both dolls, and although Black children responded similarly, for neither of the dolls was the proportion of success statistically significant.

17. Litcher, J. H. and Johnson, D. W. "Changes in attitudes toward Negroes of white elementary school students after use of multiethnic readers." Journal of Educational Psychology, 60(2), 1969, 148-152.

The experimenters investigated the effect of curriculum materials which portrayed Blacks in a way which was contradictory to prevailing prejudices and stereotypes upon the attitudes toward Blacks of White second-graders in a Midwestern city. A pretest-posttest design controlling for the teacher, the classroom, the school, and the reading ability of the students was used. The children in the experimental group used a multiethnic reader which included characters from several racial and ethnic groups for four months. The control group used the regular reader which included only Whites. It was found that use of the multiethnic reader resulted in a marked positive change in the students' attitudes toward Blacks. (Summary of journal abstract.)

18. Lombardi, D. N. "Factors affecting changes in attitudes toward Negroes among high school students." Dissertation Abstracts, 23, 1962, 1413-1414.

The purpose of the study was to examine factors which affect changes in attitudes toward Blacks among White junior and senior high school students in an integrated setting. The students' attitude change, after having classroom contact with Blacks, was found to be significantly related to the educational level of the mother.

The higher her level of education the more likely was
the student to have a favorable attitude change. Additionally, decline in scholastic average was significantly
related to negative attitude change.

19. Meketon, B. F. "The effects of integration upon the
Negro child's responses to various tasks and upon his level
of self-esteem." Dissertation Abstracts International,
30(6-A), 1969, 2339-2340.

One purpose of the study was to test whether there were
significant differences in the ability of Black children
to respond to tasks in segregated versus integrated
classrooms and to determine whether integration, with
its assumed stress-producing and morale-lowering elements would significantly lower the Black child's feelings of self-esteem. Results showed that a hypothesis
which predicted that children in an integrated class
would achieve lower scores on each task was not supported. And, the hypothesis predicting that Black children in integrated schools would have lower self-esteem
scores than those in segregated schools was only partially supported.

20. Miller, B. N. "The effects of photographic material
portraying black Americans on the behavior of white Americans." Dissertation Abstracts International, 31(4-B),
1970(Oct), 2289.

The study was done to investigate a method for changing
attitudes and behavior toward Blacks by Whites with
little exposure to Blacks. High school students were
subjects. One-third of the students saw slides of
Blacks who were like Whites. One-third saw slides of
Blacks who were stereotyped and unlike the subjects.
The final third saw no slides. After seeing the slides,
the students were to fill out a questionnaire giving
attitudes toward Blacks and were asked if they would be
willing to do one of eight things ranging from having
their picture taken with a Black person to counting
responses. Some of the findings were that subjects
seeing slides that were considered to be humanizing
felt more positive toward Blacks, while those seeing
the stereotyped slides felt sorry for Blacks.

21. Morland, J. K. "Racial recognition by nursery school
children in Lynchburg, Virginia." Social Forces, 37, 1958,
132-137.

White and Black nursery school children were given a
picture test designed to measure their ability to recognize Blacks and Whites. They were found to vary in this
ability by age and race, but not by sex or by status for
White children. Recognition ability increased regularly
with age and racial self-recognition ability was significantly higher for White children. (Summary of journal
abstract.)

22. Quinn, O. W. "The transmission of racial attitudes
among white southerners." Social Forces, 33, 1954, 41-46.

Quinn was interested in discovering the mechanisms of
transmission of racial attitudes among White southerners.
She studied the forces which transmit the philosophy of
race to the White child and found that attitudes were
not so much transmitted by verbal instruction as by the
provision of the kinds of experiences in which the child
learns behavior appropriate to his racial role and also
by shielding the child from experiences which might
teach him inappropriate roles.

23. Spencer, M. B. and Horowitz, F. D. "Effects of systematic social and token reenforcement on the modification of
racial and color concept attitudes in black and white preschool children." Developmental Psychology, 9, 1973(Sep),
246-254.

Spencer and Horowitz investigated previous findings that
preschool children negatively perceived the color black
and Black people and positively perceived the color
white and White people. Black and White Head-Start
Children were subjects. Black and white puppets were
used as stimuli. The results showed that the children
had negative attitudes toward Black people and the
color black.

24. Stern, D. and Pallone, N. J. "Effects of brief exposure
to photographic versus prose reporting of racial aggression
or harmony upon certain racial attitudes." Journal of
Social Psychology, 85, 1971, 93-101.

The purpose of the study was to investigate the effects
of prose versus prose with photographic illustration in
reporting racial aggression or harmony upon the racial
attitudes of White, middle-class adolescents. It was
found that the subjects who were low in hostility perceived less social distance between themselves and
Blacks, valued Blacks more highly, and regarded them
as more powerful regardless of what was learned about
Blacks or whether the information was communicated in
prose or illustrated prose. The racial attitudes of
subjects who were high in hostility became more negative when aggressive content was communicated and
became more positive when harmonious content was given.

25. Stern, E. G. and MacLennan, B. W. "Integrating minority
and majority youth: A socio-drama group as a human relations model." Journal of Non-White Concerns in Personnel
and Guidance, 2(3), 1974(Apr), 146-155.

Stern and MacLennan described the use of a socio-drama
group to improve human relations in schools affected by
desegregation. A social perceptions inventory was given
twice to the racially mixed group in order to determine

whether acceptance of each other within the group was
extended to racial attitudes outside the group. The
results of the first inventory showed that the attitudes
of White students were more positive than Blacks regarding integration in various situations. However, on the
the second inventory these attitudes were reversed.
Stern and MacLennan attributed this change to a confrontation which had occurred in the school prior to
the second inventory.

26. Taylor, C. P. "Some changes in self-concept in the first
year of desegregated schooling: The outward walls and the
inward scars." Dissertation Abstracts, 29(3-A), 1968, 821-
822.

The purpose of the study was to ascertain self-concept
adjustments as a result of participation in a newly
desegregated school. The results were that Black and
White children showed significantly different self-
concepts in terms of dependency, individuation, power,
and centrality. Additionally, Black students tended to
decrease in self-esteem following an initial rise, and
White students tended to increase in centrality following an initial decrement.

27. Trubowitz, J. "The effect of an activity group program
on interracial attitudes." Dissertation Abstracts International, 31(1-A), 1970(Jul), 470.

The purpose of the study was to determine the effectiveness of a school activity group program in inducing
positive changes in the racial attitudes of Black and
White New York elementary school children. A field trip
and a discussion were the methods used for interracial
contact. It was predicted that students experiencing
interracial contact, the trip contact, and the discussion would have the more positive racial attitudes.
None of the predictions were supported for fourth-grade
students. However, fifth-grade Black students experiencing the trip and discussion showed a more positive
change of attitude.

28. Whitmore, P. G. "A study of school desegregation:
Attitude change and scale validation." Dissertation
Abstracts, 17, 1957, 891-892.

A scale measuring attitudes toward Blacks was administered to White junior and senior high school students
after a period of desegregation. It was found that
students tested after desegregation had significantly
more favorable attitudes than those tested before
desegregation.

29. Williams, J. E. and Edwards, C. D. "An exploratory
study of the modification of color and racial concept attitudes in preschool children." Child Development, 40(3),
1969, 737-750.

Reinforcement procedures (giving candy or withdrawing pennies) were used to weaken the attitudes toward the concepts black and white among five-year-old White kindergarten students in the South. The results showed some reduction in the tendency to evaluate pictures of Blacks negatively and to evaluate pictures of Whites positively.

30. Williams, R. L., Cormier, W. H., Sapp, G. L., and Andrews, H. B. "The utility of behavior management techniques in changing interracial behaviors." Journal of Psychology, 77(1), 1971(Jan), 127-138.

The study was conducted to appraise the efficacy of five behavior management procedures: peer reinforcement, contingent teacher reinforcement, role modeling, group reinforcement counseling, and a control condition in changing interracial behaviors. Black and White junior high school students were subjects. The results showed a positive change on the sociometric and behavioral measures; however, the difference between the groups with regard to this change was not significant. Nevertheless, the raw data suggested that the students who had not been exposed to the experimental procedure (the control group) made the least improvement.

31. Yarrow, M. R., Campbell, J. D., and Yarrow, L. J. "Acquisition of new norms: A study of racial desegregation." Journal of Social Issues, 14(1), 1958, 8-28.

The study involved the investigation of the effects of imposed desegregation on children in a summer camp over a two-week period. The question raised was: To what extent does the changed social environment bring about changes in individuals and in group functioning and at what levels of response does conformity or nonconformity to situational expectations take place? In this paper the experimenters presented the progression of one of the groups of children in order to provide a detailed account of situational variables and contact processes. At the end of the camp experience it was found that the children tended to have favorable attitudes toward desegregation.

32. Yawkey, T. D. "Attitudes toward black Americans held by rural and urban white early childhood subjects based upon multi-ethnic studies materials." Journal of Negro Education, 42(2), 1973(Spr), 164-169.

The purpose of the study was to determine whether the attitudes of White children aged seven and seven and one-half toward Blacks could be changed through multi-ethnic social studies materials. It was found that reading and discussing selected materials by the teacher and the class produced a significantly favorable attitude change among urban and rural White children.

2

RACIAL ATTITUDES IN
YOUNG PEOPLE

33. Ammons, R. B. "Reactions in a projective doll-play
interview of white males two to six years of age to differences in skin color and facial features." Journal of
Genetic Psychology, 76, 1950, 323-341.

The experimenter used a doll-play interview method in
order to answer the following with regard to male children two to six years of age: (1) what is the course of
development of awareness of racial differences in skin
color and facial features from younger to older age
groups? and (2) how are differential social reactions
to perceived racial differences developed? The study
also included an evaluation of the doll-play interview
as a method in research. The children were tested in
public school, kindergarten, and in public day-care centers. Participation was limited to boys with at least a
two-generation "native white" background. All interviews took place in a small, unfurnished room. A black
and a white representative pipe cleaner male doll were
the stimuli along with a miniature equipped playground.
Heads with painted features were stapled to the pipe
cleaners. Fifteen questions concerning the dolls and
their activities in the playground were asked. After
six to 14 days, a second interview session was held following the same procedure. Some of the reported results
were that there was no consistent age change in favorableness of response toward either of the dolls and only
a slight change in a negative direction between sessions;
and 60 percent of the entire group identified skin color
and facial differences between the dolls, including two
of the youngest children and five of the three-year-olds.

34. Asher, S. R. and Allen, V. L. "Racial preference and
social comparison processes." Journal of Social Issues,
25(1), 1969, 157-166.

The study was a partial replication and extension of the
work by Clark and Clark (1947) on Black children's racial
preferences. The present study used both Black and White
subjects ranging in age from three to eight and divided
into middle and lower classes according to their parents'
occupations. The subjects were also grouped into age
categories: three-four, five-six, and seven-eight. The

study tested two theoretical approaches--the social comparison theory by Festinger, 1954, and a theory of social
and economic progress which stated that success experiences and extension of control over the environment create enhanced feelings of competence and racial pride.
Two same sex puppets (one black and one white) were
placed in a prone position before the subject. Two male
experimenters (one White, one Black) were used, and each
tested children of his own race. Questions adapted from
the Clark and Clark (1947) study were asked. Results
were that social class did not produce a substantial difference on any of the questions for Black children; however, on all four items, middle-class children responded
slightly more toward the white puppet. Social class made
little difference among White subjects. Concerning sex
differences, for racial preference, boys preferred the
white puppet more than did girls. Age trends showed that
for the item "play with" Black children showed a significant white preference increase from age group three-four
to five-six and then decreased at seven-eight. For White
subjects and the item "nice color," there was an increase
in white preference from age groups three-four to five-
six and a decrease at seven-eight. A historical comparison indicated an increase in white preference among Black
children. The experimenter noted that the results of the
study supported the social comparison model such that
enhanced status did not necessarily lead to greater
racial pride, but instead contributed to increased
feelings of inferiority through more frequent comparison with Whites.

35. Ball, P. M. and Cantor, G. N. "White boys' ratings of
pictures of whites and blacks as related to amount of familiarization." Perceptual and Motor Skills, 39, 1974, 883-890.

Fourth- and fifth-grade White boys were shown photographs
of White and Black boys which were presented 1, 5, 10 or
20 times. The children rated these pictures plus two
(one White, one Black) not previously exposed on a scale
indicating the extent to which they "would like to bring
the boy home to spend some time with them and their families." The black pictures were rated more favorably
than the white pictures, and increasing familiarization
was associated with an increase in favorability for black
pictures but a decrease for white pictures. (Summary of
journal abstract.)

36. Bankart, C. P. "Attribution of motivation in same-race
and different-race stimulus persons." Human Relations,
25(1), 1972(Feb), 35-45.

The purpose of the study was to test the prediction that
subjects would be less governed by stereotypes in a person perception task and therefore would be more responsive to the behavioral cues of apparent motivation in
same-race stimulus people than they would be in different-race stimulus people. Black and White male high

school and college students, respectively, were subjects.
The results showed that the hypothesis could not be supported. The descriptions of the Black person were that
he was friendly, likable, casual, and lazy, and were
ascribed by both races of subjects. Additionally, Black
subjects did not view the White stimulus person any differently than the White subjects.

37. Banks, W. C. and Rompf, W. J. "Evaluative bias and preference behavior in black and white children." Child Development, 44(4), 1973, 776-783.

Banks and Rompf attempted to reexamine self-rejection in
Blacks by requiring Black and White children to view the
performance of one Black and one White player in a ball-
tossing game. Each subject was also in the presence of
an experimenter who was either White or Black. Results
showed that, consistent with past research, White children preferred the White player, rewarded him for his
performance, and selected him as the overall winner.
Black children rewarded the White player more than the
Black player, but chose the Black player as the overall
winner. No consistent preference for Whites by the
Black subjects was shown to indicate global self-
rejection.

38. Bernard, V. W. "School desegregation: Some psychiatric
implications." Psychiatry, 21, 1958, 149-158.

Bernard discussed some of the psychological problems
entailed for Black and White students who were eligible
for or who experienced school integration after the
Supreme Court decision against segregation by May,
1954. (Summary of journal abstract.)

39. "Black and white sets." Human Behavior, 1(5), 1972, 54.

Fifth- and sixth-grade children in Michigan were asked
to name the television performers they wanted to be like.
Both Black and White children wanted to be like Diahann
Carroll and Bill Cosby. Black children spent a great
portion of television-watching-time watching the Black
shows which were televised at the time of the study.
Twenty-one percent of the White children watched these
shows. White youngsters seemed to be hesitant to say
that one race differed from another, but Blacks constantly gave a racial response to questions indicating
that they thought their race was better.

40. Blakely, K. B. and Somerville, A. W. "An investigation
of preference for racial identification terms among Negro
and Caucasion children." Journal of Negro Education, 39(4),
1970(Fal), 314-319.

The experimenters studied preferences for the terms
"Negro," "Black," "colored," "Afro-American," "White,"

and "Caucasian" among Black and White six- to 18-year
olds from low-middle- and middle-class backgrounds. The
subjects were divided into four groups according to
grades. Groups II to IV were given a question on which
to indicate their preferences and the reason for their
choice. The questions also had a "none of these" category. Subjects in group I were tested individually and
were not given the no choice option. Results showed that
there were no significant differences by sex. All subjects avoided using terms pertaining to color when referring to Blacks. Nearly three-fourths preferred to use
the terms "Negro" or "Afro-American." The same tendency
was not found for the White subjects. Although one-
fourth of the Black subjects chose the term "White,"
half of the White subjects chose this term. Although
there was also no large difference on the basis of race
or grade, certain patterns were found. White children
in grades four-six chose the anthropological term
"Negro"; but when referring to their own race chose the
term "White." At this same grade level, Black children
chose "Caucasian" and "Negro."

41. Bradley, L., Snyder, C. R., and Katahn, M. "The effects
of subject race and sex and experimenter race upon classroom-
related risk-taking behavior." Psychonomic Science, 28(6),
1972(Sep), 362-364.

Black and White students were put into a classroom test-
taking environment and were required to compete against
a comparison level (poor, average, or superior) of their
choice. The choice of a comparison level was assumed to
be equivalent to risk-taking behavior. The findings were
that students showed more risk taking by choosing a higher
comparison level when in the presence of an experimenter
of their own race. And, White male subjects showed more
risk taking than did Black males, and Black females
showed more risk taking than White females.

42. Brigham, J. C. "Views of black and white children concerning the distribution of personality characteristics."
Journal of Personality, 42(1), 1974, 144-158.

The purpose of the study was to provide evidence concerning patterns between and within the Black and White races
in the attribution of stereotype-relevant traits for
children of differing ages. Responses were obtained from
school children in grades four through 12 in two segregated Deep South schools. It was hypothesized that
within-race agreement on traits would be greater for
White than Black subjects and that within-race agreement
would be greater for older than younger children of both
races. A questionnaire designed to assess which of 50
specific traits were more characteristic of Whites or
Blacks was administered. About one year later some of
the subjects were asked to rate, for each trait, how
much they would like someone (race unspecified) with

that trait. Results showed that White subjects were consistent across grade levels in their direction of attribution to Whites and Blacks for 21 of the 50 traits (13 to Whites and eight to Blacks). Black subjects were consistent in attributing only two traits (selfish and cruel) to Whites and attributed 17 traits consistently to Blacks. The hypotheses concerning age, race, and within-group agreement were confirmed. Lastly, White subjects were found to use a "No difference" response significantly more often than did Black subjects when responding to the traits.

43. Brown, G. and Johnson, S. P. "The attribution of behavioral connotations to shaded and white figures by Caucasian children." British Journal of Social and Clinical Psychology, 10(4), 1971(Dec), 306-312.

The experimenters tested the hypothesis that with increasing age White children more frequently attribute positive behavioral characteristics to non-shaded figures and negative characteristics to shaded figures of humans. Second- and third-grade children were subjects, and each child was tested individually. The materials consisted of two cards, each with two figures of boys or girls, one shaded gray, one not. Stories were told about the boys and girls in general, and the subjects were to chose which of the two had performed the act described in the story. The card with the boys on it was shown first with its accompanying stories and then the card with the girls and their stories was shown. In each case the first and third statements referred to some negative behavior, while the second and fourth referred to positive behavior. Results showed that with age there was an increasing tendency to attribute positive statements to the non-shaded figures and negative statements to the shaded figures. There were no significant sex differences except for the seven to 7.11 age group in which males showed a greater number of prejudice choices. After age eight, there was a decrease in prejudice scores. Subjects between six and 10.11 years who came from schools with high immigrant concentrations scored in less prejudice ways.

44. Bryant, E. C., Gardner, I., Jr., and Goldman, M. "Responses on racial attitudes as affected by interviewers of different ethnic groups." Journal of Social Psychology, 70(1), 1966, 95-100.

The study was done to examine responses given to a Black and a White interviewer by Black and White adolescents. The interviewers were two Black undergraduates and two White graduate students. One Black and one White interviewer each interviewed 15 Black students. The other two interviewed 15 White students. The questions asked were concerned with social relationships between Blacks and Whites. Results showed that Black subjects were

more accepting or less prejudiced toward Whites than White
subjects were toward Blacks. Little support was found
for the hypothesis that the two groups of subjects would
shift differentially to the two types of interviewers.
And, lastly, some support was found for the hypothesis
that subjects would shift to a less prejudiced response
when answering questions about a different racial group
when interviewed by a member of the race in question.

45. Burkett, LeG. S. "Race, ethnic attitude and verbal
interaction behavior." Dissertation Abstracts International,
30(8-B), 1970(Feb), 3862.

The study assessed the effects of the race of the interviewer upon the non-content verbal behavior of Black and
White high school students and the role of the racial
prejudice of the subject in determining these effects.
Subjects were divided into high and low prejudice groups
and were interviewed by a Black or a White interviewer.
It was found that highly prejudiced subjects talked less
to the interviewer of a different race than did low-
prejudiced subjects. Additionally, when the interviewer
was of the same race, White, high-prejudiced subjects
talked more than low-prejudiced subjects. The reverse
was true for Black subjects.

46. Burrell, L. and Rayden, N. F. "Black and white students'
attitudes toward white counselors." Journal of Negro Education, 40, 1971, 48-52.

The paper reported the findings of a study designed to
examine Black and White high school students' reactions
to White counselors. Subjects came from the senior class
of an integrated city high school. The subjects were
asked to respond to 12 attitudinal items concerning their
attitudes toward their counseling experience. Results
were that the most favorable ratings came from White
males, followed by White females, Black males, and Black
females. Responses taken together indicated that only
slightly over one-half of the subjects gave favorable
responses.

47. Cantor, G. N. "Use of a conflict paradigm to study race
awareness in children." Child Development, 43(4), 1972(Dec),
1437-1442.

White elementary school children chose from among six
pairs of pictures of males in same-race or mixed-race
pairs. The children were to choose the boy in the pair
who was good and the one who was bad. For the mixed-
race pairs, subjects tended to choose the White boy for
good and the Black boy for bad.

48. Cantor, G. N. and Paternite, C. E. "A follow-up study
of race awareness using a conflict paradigm." Child Development, 44(4), 1973(Dec), 859-861.

Cantor and Paternite reported that results from an earlier conflict-paradigm study indicating the presence of
negative attitudes toward Blacks among White elementary
school children were not replicated. Pictures of same-
race or mixed-race pairs of Black and White males or
females were shown to the children. In the present study
the subjects took longer to choose a child they thought
would do something bad than one who would do something
good regardless of the racial composition of the picture
pair. Additionally, the tendency to choose the picture
of the White child for good and the picture of the Black
for bad was not evident in this study.

49. Clark, K. B. and Clark, M. P. "Racial identification
and preference in Negro children." In Readings in Social
Psychology, 3d ed., Eleanor E. Maccoby, Theodore M. Newcourt,
and Eugene L. Hartley (Eds.). New York: Henry Holt and Co.,
1958. Pp. 602-611.

The experimenters analyzed the genesis and development
of racial identification as a function of ego development
and self-awareness in Black southern and northern nursery
and public school children aged three to seven. The subjects were presented with four dolls, identical in every
way except skin color. Two of the dolls were brown with
black hair and two were white with yellow hair. All wore
white diapers. Eight questions concerning preferences
and racial identification were asked of them. Results
for preferences showed that the majority of the children
preferred the white doll. In reference to preferences
and subject's skin color, results showed that while all
subjects preferred the white dolls, the light-skinned
subjects tended to prefer them most and dark-skinned subjects preferred them least. In terms of regional differences, northern subjects generally preferred the white
doll more than did southern subjects.

50. Clarke, R. B. and Campbell, D. T. "A demonstration of
bias in estimates of Negro ability." Journal of Abnormal
and Social Psychology, 51, 1955, 585-588.

Clarke and Campbell found that estimates of the probable
performance of classmates on a forthcoming exam made in
a Black and White junior high school class showed a systematic bias or error on the part of White students
toward Black students. Black students were expected to
do worse than they actually did. (Summary of journal
abstract.)

51. Claye, C. M. "A study of the relationship between self-
concepts and attitudes toward the Negro among secondary
school pupils in three schools of Arkansas." Dissertation
Abstracts, 19, 1958, 587.

The study investigated the magnitude of the relationship
between self-concepts and attitudes toward Blacks among

secondary school children in Arkansas. Three schools
were studied: one integrated and two segregated schools.
The hypotheses were that attitudes toward Blacks were
related to one's self-concept, there would be a positive
change in attitudes toward Blacks as pupils progressed
through secondary schools (changes in self-concept would
accompany this), changes in positive attitudes toward
Blacks would accelerate with contact with Blacks in integrated schools, and there would be a positive correlation
between the ratio of Blacks to Whites in a segregated
situation and positive changes in attitudes toward Blacks.
Students from the seventh, ninth, and twelfth grades were
tested on the Tennessee Department of Mental Health Self-
Concept Scale and the Purdue University Scale for Measuring Attitudes Toward Ethnic and National Groups. The
results were that all hypotheses were rejected. Specific findings were that most of the subjects had positive self-concepts, prejudice was widespread regardless
of the number of Blacks in any situation, and contact
with Blacks had no effect on the development of positive
attitudes toward them as children progressed through
school.

52. Cohen, E. G.   "Interracial interaction disability."
Human Relations, 25(1), 1972(Feb), 9-24.

Cohen observed groups of four boys in the seventh and
eighth grades as they played a game of strategy requiring certain decisions as to which way they would proceed
on a game board. Each group was made up of two Black
and two White youngsters matched on height, socioeconomic status, and school attitude. The following predictions were supported: White boys had a higher rank
order in the group than Black boys; Whites were more
influential in decision making than Blacks, especially
when decisions were contested; and indices of influence
and rate of initiation were strongly positively related.

53. Crockett, H. J., Jr.   "A study of some factors affecting
the decision of Negro high school students to enroll in previously all white high schools, St. Louis, 1955."   Social
Forces, 35, 1957, 351-356.

The study was conducted to try to account for the fact
that although given the chance to transfer to a school
nearer their home but formerly reserved for Whites only,
many Black students decided to remain in their old
school. It was predicted that Black students from a
middle- or above-socioeconomic background would transfer
in significantly greater proportion than lower-socioeconomic students. A second prediction was that the
school ability of those who transferred would be higher
than those who remained. These hypotheses were not
supported. However, it was found that females transferred at a significantly higher rate than males in
the freshman, sophomore, and junior grades.

54. Datcher, E., Savage, J. E., and Checkosky, S. F. "School type, grade, sex, and race of experimenter as determinants of the racial preference and awareness in black and white children." Proceedings, 81st Annual Convention, American Psychological Association, Montreal, Canada, 8, 1973, 223-224.

The experimenters conducted an extension of previous research on children's racial preferences using the Clarks' doll technique which found that Black and White children preferred dolls of their own race. The present study included age, race, sex, type of school, and race of experimenter as variables. Black and White kindergarten, third-, and fifth-grade suburban children from racially segregated and mixed schools were subjects. Ten female experimenters (five Black and five White) administered the test to the subjects. The two brown and two white dolls used were identical in every way except coloring and were clothed in only a white diaper and a short white top. The questions used by Clark and Clark were used here to obtain information about racial preferences and identification and self-identification. Each subject was tested individually and was asked to respond to each question by choosing a doll. The results showed that (1) a majority of the Black children preferred the black doll; (2) most of the Black subjects made correct racial identifications; (3) type of school did not significantly influence racial preference for Black children; (4) no significant overall grade influence was found; (5) the effect of grade was significant for Black males in that higher own-race preference scores were found for older than younger males--no such effect was found for Black females; (6) the race of the experimenter had no significant effect on the Black preference score for either race of children, however, a race of experimenter X sex of subject interaction approached significance with Black males tested by a Black experimenter receiving higher Black preference scores; and (7) a significant school type X grade X race of experimenter interaction was found such that in mixed schools at the kindergarten level the Black preference score was higher with Black experimenters than with White experimenters.

55. Dienstbier, R. A. "Positive and negative prejudice: Interactions of prejudice with race and social desirability." Journal of Personality, 38(2), 1970, 198-215.

The purpose of the study was to investigate positive prejudice and its underlying dynamics. Positive Black prejudice was defined as existing when a Black stimulus person received less negative discrimination on a specific social distance dimension than a White stimulus person. In study I, male high school juniors (78 White and two Black) from middle-class families were subjects. Each read and evaluated two personality profiles, one concerning a Black and one a White male who either had

beliefs and values which were socially desirable or were
not. Subjects who were given the desirable profile as
belonging to a White individual were given an undesirable
one as belonging to a Black individual. Profiles and
race were counterbalanced across remaining subjects.
After reading and evaluating the profiles, subjects
filled out social distance measures including 16 behavioral differential scales. Results were that the more
desirable profile received higher ratings thus making
positive Black prejudice occur when the Black stimulus
person was described positively. Additionally, it was
found that overall ratings for the two profiles were
lower if the positive profile was presented first and
higher if the negative profile was presented first. In
study II, female college students known to have liberal
social and racial attitudes were subjects. A similar
format of profiles and evaluations were used, and female
stimulus persons were described. In addition to this
task, subjects were given measures of dogmatism, rigidity, and nine attitude scales concerning the Vietnam War,
crime, and rioting. The results showed that dogmatism,
rigidity, and attitudes associated with authoritarianism
were negatively related to positive prejudice.

56. Donahue, E. M. "A study of the preference of Negro and
white kindergarten children for picture book stories which
feature Negro and white story characters." Dissertation
Abstracts International, 30(10-A), 1970, 4138.

The purpose of the investigation was to compare the
responses of Black and White kindergarten boys and girls
to picture storybooks which were read to them by the
experimenter. The findings were that there was no significant difference between the preferences of the boys
and girls for books featuring Black and White story
characters.

57. Dwyer, R. J. "A report on patterns of interaction in
desegregated schools." Journal of Educational Sociology,
31, 1958, 253-256.

Dwyer noted conclusions based on observations of Black-
White student interactions in a study of seven school
districts in central Missouri where desegregation had
occurred. The results of the study were related to
propositions suggested by three other experimenters.
The following conclusions were made: (1) the lower the
grade level and age of the students the more they adjust
to integration; (2) boys adjust more readily than girls;
(3) there are more informal associations on the elementary level than on the secondary level; (4) an individual's definition of interaction in one situation as
appropriate is no indication of his feelings or behavior in another situation; and the longer an integrated
situation continues, the more likely it is that there
will be an increase in interactions.

58. Edwards, C. D. and Williams, J. E. "Generalization between evaluative words associated with racial figures in preschool children." Journal of Experimental Research in Personality, 4(2), 1970, 144-155.

Edwards and Williams reviewed the literature which has investigated the development of the evaluative dimension of connotative meaning in preschool children and which have explored the usefulness of this dimension as an assessment of racial attitudes. They used reinforcement procedures to weaken the associations of Whites as good and Blacks as bad. Then, semantic generalization was tested to positive evaluative adjectives or negative evaluative adjectives not used during training. The results were that reinforced students showed fewer customary responses during generalization than students who had not been reinforced. (Summary of journal abstract.)

59. Eppes, J. W. "The effect of varying the race of the experimenter on the level of aspiration of externally controlled inner city school children." Dissertation Abstracts International, 31(2-B), 1970(Aug), 912.

The purpose of the investigation was to examine differences between Black and White lower-socioeconomic status seventh-graders in their expectancies that events are internally or externally controlled. The race of the experimenter was varied for all of the measures given to the students. The results showed that Black students had greater expectancy for external control for one measure. Subjects who were classified as high external controllers, regardless of race or sex, did less well in school. And, subjects behaved more unrealistically and less adaptively on the Level of Aspiration measure when tested by a Black experimenter.

60. Epstein, R. and Komorita, S. S. "Prejudice among Negro children as related to parental ethnocentrism and punitiveness." Journal of Personality and Social Psychology, 4(6), 1966, 643-647.

The aim of the study was to investigate the relationship between parental punitiveness and the perceptions of parental social attitudes and social distance attitudes of Black children. The results showed that strong self-rejection existed among Black children which may have mirrored the prejudices of the white majority. Correlations between social distance scores toward their own race and toward other racial groups suggested a generalized predisposition. And, correlations between a child's social distance score and his perceptions of his parent's social distance suggested that the predispositions or attitudes were learned at home.

61. Epstein, Y. M., Krupat, E., and Obudho, C. E. "Clean is beautiful: The effects of race and cleanliness in racial

preferences."   In <u>Readings and Conversations in Social Psychology: Psychology Is Social</u>, Edward Krupat (Ed.).   Glen-
view, Illinois: Scott, Foresman and Company, 1975, 342p.

   The purpose of the study was to replicate the Clark and
   Clark (1947) experiment and to extend it to include more
   than the racial dimension to determine if other dimensions outweighed race in eliciting children's preferences
   for color pictures of Black and White children.   The
   other dimension used was the cleanliness of the child in
   the stimulus picture.   It was predicted that race rather
   than cleanliness would be the prime determinant of identification, while cleanliness rather than race would be
   the more salient determinant of preference.   A further
   concern of the study was whether own attitudes and perceived other race attitudes toward one's own race were
   balanced.   The subjects were Black and White second-,
   third-, and fourth-grade children from a school in New
   York City.   Three White and three Black female experimenters administered the eight modified Clark and Clark
   questions.   Additionally, the names and race of each
   subject's three best friends at school were obtained.
   Results showed that the most desirable situation was the
   clean child of the subject's own race, and in the absence
   of this situation both races of subjects preferred a
   clean child of the other race to a dirty child of their
   own race.   In terms of perceptions, it was found that
   perceived preferences coincided with the other race's
   actual preferences, while underestimating the degree of
   favorability the other race actually displayed.

62. Evans, C. L.   "The immediate effects of classroom integration on the academic progress, self-concept, and racial
attitude of Negro elementary children."   <u>Dissertation
Abstracts International</u>, 30(11-A), 1970(May), 4825-4826.

   The purpose of the study was to measure the effects of
   one year of school integration on Black students in
   terms of self-concept, academic achievement, and racial
   attitude.   The responses of the integrated children were
   compared with those of a group of <u>de facto</u> segregated
   Black children.   The findings were that the integrated
   students did not exceed the segregated students in academic growth.   For self-concept, segregated children
   differed from integrated children in that the latter
   loss mean points on the self-concept measure.   And for
   racial attitudes, the attitudes of segregated students
   became more positive than those of the integrated
   students.

63. Farber, R. and Schmeidler, G.   "Race differences in children's responses to 'black' and 'white.'"   <u>Perceptual and
Motor Skills</u>, 33(2), 1971(Oct), 359-363.

   Black and White seventh-graders were required to make
   line drawings and semantic differential responses to

color names, including black and white. As was predicted,
Black children evaluated the word black more favorably
than did White children. White children with better reading ability evaluated the word black less favorably.
Black children drew white with simpler, heavier, more
downward lines than did White children. They, in turn,
drew black with smaller, lighter, and more upward lines.
Farber and Schmeidler suggested that line drawings might
be used as a non-verbal measure of attitudes.

64. Fox, D. J. and Jordan, V. B. "Racial preference and
identification of black, American, Chinese, and white children." Genetic Psychology Monographs, 88(2), 1973(Nov),
229-286.

The purpose of the study was to determine the current
validity of the Clark and Clark racial preference and
identification findings with Black children. The study
by Fox and Jordan included American-Chinese, White, and
Black elementary school children from integrated or
segregated schools in New York City. Some of the
results were that most of the Black children preferred
and identified with their own racial group in contrast
to the Clarks' findings. Black and White children
showed similar own-race responses, while Chinese children showed significantly less own-race choices.

65. Frenkel-Brunswik, E. and Havel, J. "Prejudice in the
interviews of children: I. Attitudes toward minority
groups." Journal of Genetic Psychology, 82, 1953, 91-136.

The report was one of several aspects of a project dealing with social discrimination in children and concerned
their attitude towards Blacks, Mexicans, Japanese, Jews,
and foreigners in general. Disagreement with statements
about these groups was used as a measure of prejudice.
Children from three schools in northern California were
interviewed. Overall intuitive or judgmental ratings of
prejudice were made by one of the experimenters and were
done on a seven-point scale. Results showed that a
majority of the subjects were prejudiced rather than
tolerant. The highest percentage of prejudiced responses
as judged on the seven-point scale was for Blacks.
According to ethnocentrism scores, almost all of the
high scores expressed prejudice against Blacks, and only
about half of this group made prejudiced statements about
other minorities. Low scorers were relatively consistent
in the proportion of the group making prejudiced statements and those making tolerant statements. For each
minority about one-fifth made prejudiced statements,
while about one-half made tolerant ones. When "openness
of the admission of prejudice" was examined, it was found
that prejudice was openly faced most often against Mexicans and Jews, less often against Blacks and Japanese,
and not at all against Chinese. The subjects were also
found to express some of the usual stereotypes about

Blacks (lazy, conspicuous display of clothes and cars,
jealous of Whites, aggressive, physically powerful, etc.).
It was found that many of the children favored segregation. Lastly, it was noted that although the data were
"somewhat scant in this respect," correlations between
the subjects' and their parents' prejudice pointed in
the direction of family influences in ethnic tolerance
or intolerance.

66. "Friendly mixing." Human Behavior, 1(5), 1972, 52.

The article reported the results of a survey by Joseph
Gastright of the University of Cincinnati and Leon Smith
of Yeshiva University that Black students at a newly
integrated junior high school could accept the higher
academic standards with help from friendly White students. Friendship was crucial. Those students who were
felt to be bolstered by friendship, tended not to get
caught up in teachers' prejudicial attitudes or defeated
by difficult school work. However, no matter how many
Black friends White students had, they were nevertheless
anxious about their teachers' attitudes and the quality
of education they would receive.

67. Funk, J. E. "Skin color as a body image measure."
Dissertation Abstracts International, 30(7-B), 1970, 3385.

The study investigated skin color as a psychological measure. White males and females at an all White metropolitan high school were subjects and were to pick from
colors representing white and black skin tones. Among
the results was the finding that the students preferred
darker skin colors and felt them to be more attractive,
and skin color preferences and choices were related to
scores on the California F Scale (a measure of authoritarianism).

68. Geiger, O. G. "Effects of desegregation on classroom
achievement." Dissertation Abstracts, 29(11-B), 1969, 4399.

The aim of the study was to test the effects of desegregation on classroom achievement. Students from tenth-
and eleventh-grade classes at a high school in a southern metropolitan community were subjects. The results
were that there was no significant difference between
groups in terms of the amount of achievement gain over
the school year and no significant relationship between
degree of desegregation and amount of achievement gain.

69. Goodman, M. A. Race Awareness in Young Children. Cam-
bridge, Massachusetts: Addison-Wesley Press, 1952.

The purpose of the study was to investigate the awareness of race differences among Black and White three- to
five-year-olds and their feelings about these differences. The data were collected from observations,

interviews, tests, and school records. The results were
that White four-year-olds showed unmistakable signs of
the onset of social prejudice. Black children below the
age of five were aware of the differences and were uneasy
about them. Race awareness was gained from cues from
others. And the child's own physical characteristics
affected his racial responses.

70. Gordon, L. "An acculturation analysis of Negro and white
high school students: The effects on social and academic
behavior of initial close interracial association at the
secondary school level." Dissertation Abstracts, 27(8-A),
1967, 2641-2642.

The study investigated acculturation among Black and
White students in a high school program in Michigan.
The analysis consisted of examining the social and academic characteristics taken on by Black students from
White students and vice versa. It was found that Black
students participated in fewer extracurricular activities and held fewer leadership positions. Blacks showed
less preference for same-race friends and leaders than
did White students. Few Blacks were chosen as friends
by White Catholic, Jewish, and White Protestant students.
White student academic achievement continued at its high
level after the Black students were introduced to the
school. And, there was more social interaction between
Black and White males than between Black and White
females.

71. Greenberg, H., Chase, A. L., and Cannon, T. M., Jr.
"Attitudes of white and Negro high school students in a
west Texas town toward school integration." Journal of
Applied Psychology, 41, 1957, 27-31.

The aim of the study was to ascertain student attitudes
toward integrated situations and to determine whether
negative attitudes toward integration would correlate
with authoritarian attitudes. Black and White students
from segregated public high schools in west Texas were
subjects. The results showed that authoritarian attitudes of the students were not indicative of negative
attitudes toward integration; Black students in segregated schools were highly authoritarian and had strongly
positive attitudes toward school integration; White students in segregated schools were also highly authoritarian, but less so than Black students; and White students showed some positive attitudes toward many aspects
of school integration.

72. Gregor, A. J. and McPherson, D. A. "Racial attitudes
among white and Negro children in a deep south standard
metropolitan area." Journal of Social Psychology, 68,
1966, 95-106.

A variation of the Clarks' Doll Test was used to assess
racial attitudes, cognition, and identification among

Black and White children in a Deep South metropolitan
area public school. The baby dolls used were identical
in form and feature and different only in hair and skin
color. The children were shown the dolls and asked nine
questions designed to tap racial cognition, identification, and attitudes. Each subject was tested individually by an experimenter of his own race. Results for
White subjects revealed that a majority of them gave
responses in terms of in-group preference on four of the
preference questions. The subjects were also correct in
identifying the dolls by race and on the self-identification question. Results for Black subjects showed that
they made a majority of in-group choices. For the question concerning the doll that looked bad, only eight
subjects out of the sample of 92 chose to answer, and of
those who responded, all chose the black doll. Black
subjects were also correct in identifying the represented race of the dolls, and a majority of them made
a correct self-identification choice. Sex differences
for Black subjects indicated that females were more
out-group oriented than males, and more females misidentified themselves than males.

73. Halpern, F. "Self-perception of black children and the
civil rights movement." American Journal of Orthopsychiatry,
40(3), 1970(Apr), 520-526.

Halpern concluded that the civil rights movement has
touched the lives of all Black children, regardless of
the region of residence. However, how they respond to
the movement and how they experience it is dependent
upon the nature of their relation to and identification
with their families.

74. Harris, D. B., Gough, H. G., and Martin, W. E. "Children's ethnic attitudes. II. Relationship to parental
beliefs concerning child training." Child Development,
21(3), 1950(Sep), 170-181.

The purpose of the study was to explore the relationship
between the authoritarian and disciplinary attitudes of
parents in regard to child-rearing practices. Its aim
was also to explore the incidence of ethnic bias in the
children of these individuals. Questionnaires concerning child-rearing practices were sent to the mothers of
children from two sample schools. A questionnaire concerning White boys' attitudes toward Black boys were
given to the male students at these schools. The experimenters concluded that a child's prejudice is associated with parental attitudes concerning authoritarian
handling of control and a lack of tolerance of the
child's annoyance value.

75. Harris, S. and Braun, J. R. "Self-esteem and racial
preference in black children." Proceedings of the Annual
Convention of the American Psychological Association, 6
(Pt. 1), 1971, 259-260.

The purpose of the study was to examine the relationship
between self-esteem and racial preferences in Black children. It was predicted that subjects with impaired self-
concepts would be more out-group oriented than those with
unimpaired self-concepts; that middle-class subjects
would prefer Whites more than lower-class subjects; and
that there would be a significant difference between
males and females in their choice of a black or white
puppet or some racial preference statements. The results
showed that prediction one was supported; however, there
were no sex or social class differences in racial preference for the children. The majority of them preferred
the black puppet.

76. Hayes, M. L.   "Attitudes of high school students toward
Negro problems." Journal of Education Research, 46, 1953,
615-619.

The purpose of the study was to determine the attitudes
towards Blacks of adolescents in different types of
schools and in grades within the schools determined by
age, sex, intellectual level, and cultural background.
The schools were: a private girls' school with students
from high socioeconomic backgrounds, a consolidated
village-rural public school with a good socioeconomic
background, a campus school in connection with a teachers' college, a large city public school (the only
school sample with Black subjects). A part of the Social
Problems Analysis, Advanced Series, was used to determine attitudes. Results by sex showed that females
tended to have more favorable attitudes toward Black
problems than did males. By cultural group, Jewish
Americans had the most favorable attitudes, old-stock
American subjects had the next most favorable, and new-
stock American subjects had the least favorable attitudes. Interestingly, the three Black subjects in the
sample had the least favorable attitudes. By age, subjects who were the appropriate age for their grade had
more favorable attitudes than over-age subjects.
According to intelligence, subjects with higher intelligence had more favorable attitudes toward Black problems than those of lower intelligence. No sex differences were found for the high intellectual level, but at
the average level girls were more favorable toward the
problems than boys.

77. Hatton, J. M.   "Reactions of Negroes in a biracial bargaining situation." Journal of Personality and Social Psychology, 7(3, Pt. 1), 1967, 301-306.

Black high school girls who perceived Whites as highly
prejudiced against Blacks were put in a monopoly bargaining situation with Black or White confederates. The confederates adopted either a yielding or demanding bargaining strategy. The results were that subjects in
conditions in which the bargaining structure and the

subjects' attitudinal orientation was balanced (coopera-
tive-positive or competitive-negative) obtained lower
payoffs than those in conditions of imbalance (coopera-
tive-negative or competitive-positive). (Summary of
journal abstract.)

78. Hebron, M. E. and Ridley, F. "Characteristics associated
with racial prejudice in adolescent boys." British Journal
of Social and Clinical Psychology, 4(2), 1965, 92-97.

The purpose of the study was to determine the role of
self-esteem and esteem for other in-group members as
these are related to anxiety and racial prejudice toward
the English, Jews, Blacks, Norwegians, and Russians.
White adolescent boys were subjects. It was found that
self-esteem, stereotypes, and anxiety contributed to
prejudice scores. And, an unrealistic self-image in
regard to socially appropriate behavior increased the
tendency to make prejudicial judgments concerning similar traits in other nationalities.

79. Hraba, J. "The doll technique: A measure of racial
ethnocentrism." Social Forces, 50(4), 1972(Jun), 522-527.

The paper was concerned with the methodology used in
studies of racial preference among children using the
actual or modifications of the Clarks' (1947) doll technique. The question raised was: Are the four preference items unidimensional and do they measure the same
thing--racial preference? If not, which items measure
what? Black and White elementary school children in
kindergarten through second grade were subjects. Names
and race of the subjects' friends were also obtained.
Dolls were used as stimuli. Two response patterns were
investigated: (1) choosing a doll of one race for questions one, two, and four, and of the other race for
question three; and (2) choosing dolls of one race when
that choice was not popular among own-race peers, and
also choosing the same dolls on each item where that
choice was more popular. Results showed that pattern
one was evidenced in 26 and 28 percent of the Black and
White subjects, respectively. Black subjects used this
pattern more frequently with increasing age. Age was
not significantly associated with this pattern for White
subjects. Responses tended to support the second proposed pattern and suggested that children change their
preferences because they intended to express a liking
for both races. For ethnocentrism and friendship, it
was found that White subjects with more ethnocentrism
tended not to have Black friends. There was no such
trend for Black subjects. In fact, among Black subjects,
those who were more ethnocentric on doll choices tended
to have more White friends.

80. Hraba, J. and Grant, G. "Black is beautiful: A re-exam-
ination of racial prejudice and identification." Journal of
Personality and Social Psychology, 16(3), 1970(Nov), 398-402.

The experimenters tested the thesis that for Black children, interracial contact engendered preference for Whites
using the Clarks' doll technique and four- to eight-year-
old Black and White elementary school children as subjects. The same questions used by the Clarks were used
in the present study. According to results, both races
of children preferred dolls representing their own race.
This trend was found for all age groups and tended to
increase with age. The experimenters also found that
subjects with light skin color were as strong in their
preference for a black doll as were the other Black subjects. Concerning racial identification, the experimenters found that a majority of the subjects made correct
identifications of the black and white dolls. Fifteen
percent of the light-skinned subjects misidentified themselves in regard to the question concerning "the doll
that looks like you"; however, there was no significant
difference between skin tone groups in terms of misiden-
tification on this question. The experimenters concluded
with a discussion of some explanations for the lack of
relationship between doll choice and friendship choice.

81. Insko, C. A. and Robinson, J. E. "Belief similarity
versus race as determinants of reactions to Negroes in southern white adolescents: A further test of Rokeach's theory."
Journal of Personality and Social Psychology, 7(2, Pt. 1),
1967, 216-221.

Insko and Robinson tested Rokeach's belief-race theory
using ninth-grade students from a southern community.
The results showed that belief was more effective according to responses on the semantic differential, but that
race was more effective than belief according to
responses on two factor scales designed by Triandis.
(Summary of journal abstract.)

82. Johnson, D. W. "Racial attitudes of Negro freedom school
participants and Negro and white civil rights participants."
Social Forces, 45(2), 1966, 266-273.

The experimenter investigated the racial attitudes of a
group of Black children and teen-agers participating in
a Freedom School where they were taught Black history
and a militant interracial civil rights group of teen-
agers. The experimental questionnaire contained a series
of concepts dealing with attitudes toward Blacks and
Whites. Each concept was followed by four six-point
semantic differential scales using the evaluative dimension (good-bad, fair-unfair, clean-dirty, and valuable-
worthless). The subjects, in turn, evaluated the concepts as they referred to Blacks and then Whites. Next,
they evaluated the Black concepts as they thought most
Whites would. The general results were that the subjects had positive attitudes toward Blacks even though
they perceived that most Whites had negative attitudes.
Furthermore, Black civil rights subjects evaluated

Blacks and Whites equally, except for the concept
"Negroes" which was evaluated higher than the concept
"White People." White civil rights members evaluated
Blacks higher than Whites in four instances: "Negro
Man," "Negro Woman," "Negroes against Civil Rights,"
and "Negro Policeman." And, both groups of subjects
perceived Whites as having negative attitudes toward
Whites.

83. Kaalberg, R. M. "Racial preferences of second-, fourth-,
and sixth-grade Negro and Caucasian girls in hypothetical and
actual social situations." Dissertation Abstracts International, 33(7-A), 1973(Jan), 3386.

The study examined the racial preferences of elementary
school girls in the Deep South. Subjects were second-,
fourth-, and sixth-grade Black and White girls from
Catholic schools. In the first session, the children
were shown color photos of six Black and six White girls
from the same grades. Each subject was asked to select
four girls with whom she would like to eat, become better
acquainted, sit, work on a committee, and play a recre-
ational game. Each was told that she would not actually
meet the four. The responses showed racial preferences.
At a second session, about one week later, the subjects
were given an opportunity to select girls with whom they
would like to associate in an actual social situation.
In this situation the girls whose pictures were used were
present. Some results were that prejudice for racially
different girls was greater for Black subjects than for
Whites in the second and fourth grades in the hypothetical situation. Only for fourth-grade girls in the actual
situation was there no significant difference between
Blacks and Whites in this regard. There was no developmental decrease in choices of other-race girls. Second-
grade girls preferred other-race partners more in the
actual than hypothetical situation. And, a developmental
increase in difference between situations was not found.

84. Katz, I. Conflict and Harmony in an Adolescent Interracial Group. New York: New York University Press, 1955,
iii, 47p.

Katz studied a voluntary urban group of high school-age
males and females which met frequently under the sponsorship of the municipal government. The activities, factors underlying tensions, social pressures, community
approval and disapproval, and disruptive motivational
and perceptual factors were discussed. (Summary of
journal abstract.)

85. Katz, P. A., Johnson, J., and Parker, DeA. "Racial attitudes and perception in black and white urban school children." Proceedings of the Annual Convention of the American Psychological Association, 5(Pt. 1), 1970, 311-312.

The research involved a developmental study of racial
attitudes. In addition to questionnaire materials, a
projective technique was used which asked the subjects
about slides of ambiguous interracial situations with
children. Prejudice was operationally defined as the
tendency to attribute malevolent deeds and motivations
to a child of another race and the tendency to attribute
benevolent deeds and motivations to a child of the same
race. Subjects were Black and White second-, fourth-,
and sixth-graders. Black and White experimenters were
used. The other tests used were a social distance scale
using photographs of Black, White, and Oriental children;
a General Intolerance Questionnaire; a children's form of
a Dogmatism Scale assessing general political beliefs;
and a Self-Concept Scale. Results showed a decline in
prejudice with age on the social distance and general
intolerance scales which suggested that these measures
were heavily loaded with a social desirability factor.
With the projective test, no significant differences
were associated with age, race of subject or race of
experimenter. For the slides on which subjects were to
indicate the degree of similarity between pairs of children differing in color and shade within each race, it
was found that with the Black experimenter higher dis-
tinctiveness scores on all slides were obtained. The
effect of age produced increased similarity with older
subjects except with the White experimenter in which
case the pairs were seen as more different by older
children. For shade differences, second- and fourth-
graders viewed the shade differences of other races as
more distinctive than their own; however, by the sixth
grade this trend was reversed and faces of their own
race were viewed as more distinctive than others, particularly by White subjects.

86. Kircher, M. and Furby, L. "Racial preferences in young
children." Child Development, 42(6), 1971(Dec), 2076-2078.

The purpose of the study was to investigate whether children of ages three, four, and five would show preference
for features other than skin color such as eye color,
hair color, and hair type. Black and White three-, four-,
and five-year-olds were subjects. Pairs of drawings of
children's faces were shown to them. The drawings varied
in eye color (blue and brown), hair color (brown and
black), hair type (straight and curly), and skin color
(white and dark brown). Within each pair the characteristic of only one feature differed. Each subject was
tested individually and was asked to point to the picture
of the child he would rather play with. Results showed
that the typically white characteristic for hair type and
skin color was most preferred. Both races made identical
eye color and hair type choices, but Blacks tended to
prefer black hair more than did Whites; and Whites showed
slightly more preference than did Blacks for white skin.
According to an age X race analysis for hair type and

skin color, significant preferences for white characteristics were centered at age four. It was suggested that
this may have occurred because the three- and five-year-
olds had black head teachers, while the four-year-olds
had a white head teacher. As age increased, Blacks
showed more preference for blue eyes, while Whites
remained neutral. With increasing age, Blacks showed
no preference for hair color, but Whites preferred black
hair. With increasing age, Blacks and Whites preferred
straight hair. Both four- and five-year-old Whites preferred white skin. Four-year-old Blacks preferred white
skin, but by age five there was no preference. Since
three-year-old Blacks also showed no preference, the
preference of four-year-olds was suggested to be the
result of having a White teacher. The results of this
study concerning preferences for white skin with
increasing age contradicted those of other studies.

87. Koslin, S. C., Amarel, M., and Ames, N. "A distance
measure of racial attitudes in primary grade children: An
exploratory study." Psychology in the Schools, 6(4), 1969,
382-385.

The aim of the study was to design an instrument that
could be used to measure interpersonal racial attitudes
among primary school children in segregated and nonsegregated school settings. First- and second-grade
children from an all White, all Black, and a mixed race
school were subjects. The children were required to
place a figure representing themselves in whatever position and at whatever distance they wished from other
figures representing a mother, a father, a school, Black
and White teachers, and Black and White peers. It was
found that White students placed their self figure further away from the Black targets than did Black subjects.
Black children placed themselves equally close to Black
and White figures. Integrated Black children placed
themselves closer to White figures than segregated Black
children. And, integration accelerated a tendency for
White children to place themselves closer to Black children figures as grade increased.

88. Koslin, S. C., Amarel, M., and Ames, N. "The effect of
race on peer evaluation and preference in primary grade children: An exploratory study. Journal of Negro Education, 39,
1970(Fal), 346-350.

The purpose of the study was to explore the use of children's preferences for sketches of classrooms which
differed in racial composition as a measure of school-
related racial attitudes. First- and second-grade children from a middle-sized eastern city were subjects.
The children were required to point to the picture of
their choice after being asked questions concerning
classroom scenes. One picture was of a class with 10
White and two Black children and the other was of a

class with 10 Black and two White students. The results
showed that Black students divided in their preferences,
but that White students tended to choose the predominately
White classrooms.

89. Koslin, S. C., Koslin, B., Pargament, R., and Waxman, H.
"Classroom racial balance and students' interracial attitudes." Sociology of Education, 45(4), 1972, 386-407.

The purpose of the research was to study the relationship
between students' racial attitudes and the degree of
classroom level integration within desegregated schools.
The study was done in racially mixed elementary schools
using third-graders as subjects. The schools were in a
large eastern city. The following measures of racial
attitudes were used: (1) a sociometric choice measure
to determine the three classmates with whom each child
played most often in school and the three classmates each
child would most like to invite to a party at their house,
(2) a classroom preference test to determine preference
for classrooms and teachers, and (3) The People Test to
determine social distances between different types of
people. Results showed that for sociometric choices,
children in all schools tended to choose classmates of
their own race. Sex effects for sociometric choice
showed that males chose a higher proportion of Blacks in
unbalanced classrooms than in balanced ones, while girls
did the opposite. This interaction was due almost
entirely to the responses of Black males and White
females. Results for teacher preference showed that
White subjects chose White teachers most and Black subjects chose Black teachers most. However, Black subjects in balanced classes chose more White teachers than
Blacks in unbalanced classes; and Whites in balanced
classes chose more Black teachers than Whites in unbalanced classes. For classmate preferences, subjects
tended to prefer classmates of their own race, but this
polarization was less extreme in balanced than in unbalanced classes. For The People Test, subjects in balanced classes placed the self figure closer to the four
target figures than those in unbalanced classes. Race
of target effects occurred so that White subjects placed
the self closer to white targets and Blacks placed it
closer to black targets. Females placed the self closer
to female targets, regardless of race; and males placed
the self closer to male targets. Lastly, balance had an
effect so that self-target distances were always smaller
in balanced environments.

90. Krystall, E. R., Friedman, N., Howze, G., and Epps, E. G.
"Attitudes toward integration and black consciousness:
Southern Negro high school seniors and their mothers."
Phylon, 31(2), 1970(Sum), 104-113.

Results of the 1967 Tuskegee Area Study, which was an
annual social survey conducted by junior and senior

social science majors at the institute, showed that high
school seniors, as compared with their parents, were more
favorable toward integration, more strongly identified
with Blackness, and more willingly joined or participated
in a Black power movement. The parents were described as
being pro-integrationist, but not pro-Black conscious.

91. Kutner, B. and Gordon, N. B. "Cognitive functioning and
prejudice: A nine-year follow-up study." Sociometry, 27(1),
1964, 66-74.

The paper examined the stability of the patterned relationship between social attitudes and cognitive functions. Tests of reasoning and prejudice toward Blacks,
Puerto Ricans, and Jews were given to children just at
age seven and then at age 16. Results indicated a tri-
modal pattern: two groups of hard-core students at the
extremes of the prejudice pole and a group of students
who shifted in both cognitive approach and attitude.
(Summary of article abstract.)

92. Landreth, C. and Johnson, B. C. "Young children's
responses to a picture and inset test designed to reveal
reactions to persons of different skin color." Child Development, 24(1), 1953(Mar), 63-79.

The study was designed to explore the significance of
economic status and social circumstances on three- to
five-year-old White and Black children's responses to
individuals of different skin color. A picture and
inset test were given in which the choice of one of a
pair of insets had to be made to complete a picture.
Some results were that White upper-class children tended
to match by skin color. Black children tended to choose
white over black, white over brown, and brown over black
skin color. A sex difference showed that three-year-old
White upper-class girls and lower-class boys preferred
white skin more than White lower-class girls and upper-
class boys.

93. Lansman, M. "The relation of self-image to Negro
achievement and attendance in a racially integrated elementary school." Dissertation Abstracts, 29(2-A), 1968,
442-443.

Lansman attempted to find whether there was a positive
relationship between negative self-images in Black children and academic achievement level and whether there
was a positive relationship between negative self-image
and school attendance. Black and White elementary
school children were compared. The results showed that
Black children received lower achievement test scores
than White children and this result remained when
females were compared. However, there was no significant difference between Black and White males. Finally,
there was no significant difference between Black and
White attendance.

94. Lerner, R. M. and Karson, M. "Racial stereotypes of early adolescent white children." Psychological Reports, 32(2), 1973(Apr), 381-382.

White, lower-middle-class junior high school students were asked to attribute each of 48 items from a verbal checklist to a picture of a White or a Black male. The findings were that the subjects had predominantly unfavorable views of the Black male and favorable views of the White male.

95. Lewis, C. and Biber, B. "Reactions of Negro children toward Negro and white teachers." Journal of Experimental Education, 20, 1951, 97-104.

The purpose of the study was to determine whether Black children would be more influenced by color or the pleasant-unpleasant aspects of pictures when they were required to pick those which reminded them of their teachers. It also examined the extent to which color determined choice priority in the pictures they liked. Pictures of medium-dark Black and White brunet adults were used. Results showed that the children with Black teachers found it easier to see resemblances in the white pictures than did children with White teachers looking for resemblances in the black pictures. Additionally, when asked to pick the pictures they liked, children with Black teachers chose more black pictures than white. All children were influenced by the pleasant-unpleasant aspect of the faces. And, females were more ready to accept Black teachers than were boys.

96. Martelle, D. L. "Interracial marriage attitudes among high school students." Psychological Reports, 27(3), 1970 (Dec), 1007-1010.

White and Black high school students were questioned concerning whether one group favored interracial marriage more than the other. Martelle found that the Black students were more favorable toward interracial marriage than the White students; and all males tended to favor such marriages more than females.

97. Martinez-Monfort, A. "Racial attitudes of high school students attending desegregated schools in a southern metropolitan area." Dissertation Abstracts International, 31(8-A), 1972(Feb), 4972-4973.

The purpose of the study was to assess the verbal attitudes and non-verbal reactions of high school students enrolled in desegregated schools to desegregated situations. The following hypotheses were presented: (1) there would be a significant difference between the racial attitudes of the subjects who had two years or less of experience in desegregated schools and those of students with three years or more experience, (2)

physiological indicators of anxiety would be greater in
number when subjects were confronted with informal racial
contact school situations than with formal situations,
(3) physiological indicators would bear a positive relationship to the amount of experience a student had had in
a desegregated school situation, (4) Black females would
respond with more physiological indicators than would
Black males when responding to vicarious informal situations, and (5) subjects would show an increase in anxiety state variety when confronted with formal and informal slides. The subjects were given questionnaires and
paper and pencil measures of anxiety in addition to
seeing slides of vicarious situations while their physiological reaction to them were recorded. Results were
that hypotheses one, three, and five were rejected,
while two and four were accepted.

98. McClay, E. S. "A historical analysis of skin color perception and racial attitudes in black and white children."
Smith College Studies in Social Work, 44(1), 1973(Nov), 23.

The experimenter conducted a library historical study
to explore racial attitudes in Black and White children.
The predictions were that Black self-image strengthened
or weakened as periods in history changed and that Black
and White children learned to differentiate themselves
in terms of skin color perception. McClay found that
the periods between the 1900's and the 1970's had a great
affect on Black self-image and that Black and White children learned to differentiate themselves on the basis of
skin color at an early age.

99. McPartland, J. M. "The segregated student in desegregated schools: Sources of influence on Negro secondary
students." Dissertation Abstracts, 29(5-A), 1968, 1605.

The purpose of the study was to determine the effects of
different degrees of desegregation on Black students'
attitudes and academic development and to describe the
situational components of the environments which explain
the effects. An important result was that although
desegregation at the school level had a positive effect
on Black students' achievement, those who remained in
segregated classes within the school received no bene-
fits in regard to academic growth. Each of the situational factors had an effect on the students but influenced different aspects of their development.

100. Melchiode, G., Gould, S., and Fink, P. J. "Beware of
whites bearing gifts." American Journal of Psychiatry, 127,
1970(Jul-Dec), 803-808.

The paper concerned how four Black patients at a mental
health center were affected by the attempt to provide
them with an adequate education at a White private
school through a special program. The study involved

an investigation of the psychological and social stress
placed upon the individuals, the ways in which they tried
to cope with this problem, and the health center's role
in helping them. In each case the authors found a feeling of isolation and alienation on the part of the subjects. Some dropped out of the program either because
they could not keep up with the work required or because
they were pressured from friends in their own community
because they were attending such a program. It was suggested that future educational programs be created to
avoid some of the pitfalls of student selection, isolation, exaggerated racial imbalance, and arbitrary uni-
lateral development of the program. Furthermore, students with severe emotional problems should not be
placed in the program because of the stress they might
face.

101. Meltzer, B. "The influence of the duration of interracial classroom contact on the development of interpersonal
cognitive skills." Dissertation Abstracts International,
31(1-A), 1970(Jul), 467-468.

The purpose of the study was to investigate whether a
relationship exists between the degree of contact one
individual maintains with others different from himself
and the degree of maturity of skills in understanding,
evaluating, and predicting the behavior of others.
Black and White ninth-graders who had experienced different degrees of interracial classroom contact were
subjects. The students were shown films of a Black and
a White boy engaged in single or dyadic prosocial, anti-
social, or ambiguous activities. The students were to
describe, evaluate, and make predictions about the boys.
Some of the findings were that increases in the duration
of interracial contact were associated with increasing
maturity in cognitive skills. And, as a function of the
degree of contact, cognitive skills increased more for
the Black stimulus than the White stimulus.

102. Menchise, D. N. "Racial bias as a determinant of literary preference and the relationship of selected variables
to patterns of preference and rejection of literary works
whose author's race is known." Dissertation Abstracts International, 33(6-A), 1972(Dec), 2619.

The experimenter wanted to determine whether knowledge of
an author's race acted as a determinant of literary preferences and rejections of urban Black and White high
school students. The students were asked to rank 10
poems written by Black and White authors in the order of
their preference. Each poem was accompanied by the auth-
or's name and picture. Peer judges were also asked to
rank the poems, but did not receive information about
names or race. Results showed that there was a significant difference between races in the ranking of the poems
with Black subjects ranking the poems by Black authors

higher than those by White authors. White subjects did
the reverse. No sex differences or sex X race differences were found. The experimenter subsequently made
recommendations for literature and urban studies courses
based on the findings.

103. Nicholas, K. B., McCarter, R. E., and Heckel, R. V.
"The effects of race and sex on the imitation of television
models." Journal of Social Psychology, 85(2), 1971(Dec),
315-316.

The purpose of the study was to determine whether boys
would choose different models from girls, whether Blacks
would choose different models from Whites, and whether
competency of a model would increase imitation of the
model. The subjects were Black and White, male and
female second-graders who watched models on a television
set in front of the classroom. Some of the results were
that White females chose the White boy and the Black boy
model most frequently. Black females chose the Black
male model most and the White male model least.

104. Owen, I. "Adlerian counseling racially mixed groups of
elementary school children." Individual Psychologist, 7(2),
1970(Nov), 53-58.

Owen discussed the lack of experimental support for the
hypothesis that Adlerian counseling would significantly
modify negative attitudes in racially mixed groups and
for the prediction that the changes would be greater for
subjects who were counseled simultaneously by a Black and
a White counselor. Fifth- and sixth-grade Black and
White children were divided into same-race groups and
were led by either a White, a Black, or a White and a
Black counselor, or were put into a control group which
engaged in light conversation, magazine reading, or
playing records or games. (Summary of journal abstract.)

105. Paige, J. N. "Changing patterns of anti-white attitudes
among blacks." Journal of Social Issues, 26(4), 1970(Fal),
69-86.

Paige predicted that young Black males who were more
receptive to new strategies of inter-group conflict
would have higher levels of anti-White attitudes; the
old, females, and southern-born would be less prejudiced
now than the young, males, and northern-born; authoritarianism would be negatively associated with racial
pride as well as anti-White feeling; racial pride would
be positively associated with anti-White feeling; and
militancy would be positively associated with in-group
pride and anti-White feeling. An incidental sample of
Black males ranging in age from 15 to 35 from Newark,
New Jersey, were subjects. Some of the findings were
that more Black males held anti-White attitudes in 1968
than in 1949. The young were more anti-White than the

old and northern-born subjects were more anti-White than
southern-born subjects.

106. Palmer, E. L. "Color preference as a distinct forerun-
ner of color prejudice in the young child." Dissertation
Abstracts International, 31(8-A), 1971(Feb), 4265-4266.

The purpose of the study was to resolve the question concerning color preference versus racial prejudice among
three-, four-, eight-, and 10-year-old Black and White
children from racially mixed and segregated neighborhoods. The materials were a color selection table with
a sliding tray and 10 tray inserts. Five of the inserts
were rectangular wooden blocks and five were wooden gingerbread men. One of each insert was one of the following colors: red, yellow, blue, black, and flesh tone.
The subject was to pick the one he liked best from among
the two placed in the trays by an experimenter on each
trial. The black and white pair was that of importance.
Hypotheses were that color preference would prevail in
three- and four-year-olds, regardless of race or degree
of neighborhood interracial contact and that color prejudice would be found in the eight- and 10-year-olds from
segregated neighborhoods. Later subjects from mixed
neighborhoods were expected to show no change between
phases (phase one presented blocks, phase two presented
gingerbread men). Results did not confirm the initial
hypotheses; however, both races of subjects from mixed
neighborhoods registered other race preferences in phase
two. These latter results questioned Allport's view
that only Black preschool children would demonstrate
cross-racial preferences.

107. Palmer, E. L. "Color prejudice in children as a function of race, age, and residence neighborhood." Proceedings, 81st Annual Convention, American Psychological Association, 1973, 225-226.

Palmer noted that similar research findings had been
given different interpretations concerning the prefer-
ence-prejudice question. He looked at the responses of
children from public schools and day care centers on a
colored block and gingerbread man selection task as a
means of determining color "prejudice." The stimulus
was a color selection table with three rectangular tray
pockets. Built to fit the pockets were five wooden
blocks and five wooden gingerbread men in the following
colors: red, yellow, blue, black, and flesh tone white.
The subject and an experimenter were seated at opposite
ends of a table separated by a curtain. Two blocks were
placed in the outer pockets of the tray which was then
slid beneath the curtain to the subject. The subject
was to place in the middle the block he liked best and
to slide it back to the experimenter. Trials were run
with the blocks and then with the gingerbread men.
Color prejudice was defined as a significant phase two

choice shift toward the skin color of group members, and
color preference was defined as no significant phase two
shift from the base-line color preference pattern established during phase one. It was hypothesized that color
preference would occur among eight- to 10-year-olds from
racially segregated neighborhoods and that color prejudice would not occur among eight- to 10-year-olds from
racially mixed neighborhoods. Analysis of the data
showed that for the trials X race X age interaction,
choice of one race color was prominent among Black and
White four-year-olds in phase one and eight-year-olds in
phase two. Additionally, White four-year-olds from
racially mixed neighborhoods chose Blacks significantly
more during phase two than phase one, while Black four-
year-olds from racially mixed neighborhoods showed a
similar preference shift toward white color choice.
Black four-year-olds from racially segregated neighborhoods maintained a strong choice of Black in the second
phase.

108. Petroni, F. A. "Adolescent liberalism: The myth of a
generation gap." Adolescence, 7(26), 1972(Sum), 221-232.

The purpose of the paper was to challenge the assumption
that youth and adults occupy polar positions on the
issue of race relations. It was found that the assumption of generational differences in racial tolerance may
be best understood as a tendency to overgeneralize the
generation gap theory. The data were collected as part
of a study of a desegregated high school in the midwest
in which 30 percent of the students were Black, 1 percent Mexican-American, less than 1 percent Indian, and
the remainder White. Various subgroups were also identified: upper- and middle-class Whites, racists, conservatives, hippies, peaceniks, militants, and athletes,
among others. The students were interviewed with a non-
fixed choice questionnaire by White experimenters. It
was found that the subjects felt themselves to be more
liberal than adults, and even the Black militants perceived themselves to be less prejudiced against Whites
than their parents. Thus, in general, the perceived
difference between old and young was, as the experimenter noted, more apparent than real.

109. Radke, M. J. and Trager, H. G. "Children's perceptions
of the social roles of Negroes and whites." Journal of Psychology, 29, 1950, 3-33.

The experimenters studied the extent to which young children were aware of social differences and examined the
part social differences played in the development of
children's attitudes toward race. Black and White kindergarten, first-, and second-grade children in Philadelphia public schools were tested. Each child's perception of the social roles of Black and White adults
and his evaluation of members of each race were

determined through a doll-play technique and interview.
Black and white male and female plywood dolls and house
forms were the stimuli. All subjects were interviewed
with same sex dolls. The children were brought to the
test after responding to pictures of groups of children
of different races and religions at a playground. For
the doll test, subjects were shown costumes representing
dress-up, work, and shabby clothes and were asked which
one they liked best. Then, a black doll and a white doll
were presented along with identification questions and a
request to the subject to dress the dolls using any
clothes he liked and to decide which house each lived
in. The interview proceeded in this manner. Results
showed that a number of the White children assigned inferior social roles to the black dolls. Among Black subjects, 16 percent ascribed inferior roles. In dressing
the dolls, the experimenters found that the subjects generally dressed up the doll of their own race. And in
selecting houses, a majority of the children gave the
poor house to the black doll and the good house to the
white doll. In the portion of the research in which the
children were shown pictures of Black and White children
at a playground, comparisons were made between roles
ascribed and responses. It was found that not all of
the White subjects who ascribed inferior roles to Blacks
expressed hostile feelings toward them, and subjects who
showed no awareness of social distinctions in the houses
or costumes they chose expressed hostility on the picture
attitude measure in 60 percent of the cases.

110. Richardson, S. A. and Emerson, P. "Race and physical
handicap in children's preference for other children." Human
Relations, 23(1), 1970, 31-36.

The experimenters replicated a study by Richardson and
Royce (1968). In the present study, a southern city was
used in which there were segregated schools and widespread racial discrimination and prejudice. It was predicted that color would be more salient than physical
disability in determining prejudice. Black females aged
eight to 13 were subjects. The experimenters were unable
to obtain permission to conduct the same study with White
subjects. The test was administered by a White female
interviewer to each subject individually. All of the
subjects saw drawings of females. The six drawings were
placed in random order and the instructions were to indicate the picture liked best and then those in succeeding
order. This procedure was continued until a complete
ranking was obtained. The six pictures portrayed children with no physical handicap, crutches and a brace, a
wheelchair with legs covered by a blanket, left forearm
amputated, slight facial disfiguration, and obesity.
The subjects were divided into the following sets: set
one subjects were shown White children; set two saw
Black children. For these two sets, handicap was varied.
Lastly, sets three and four had color and handicap

varied. The results showed that the subjects took color
into account more often in the judgments. The subjects
were also found to show a preference for White over Black
in sets three and four.

111. Rohrer, G. K. "Racial and ethnic identification and
preference in young children." Dissertation Abstracts International, 33(7-A), 1973(Jan), 3404-3405.

The experimenter investigated racial and ethnic identification and prejudice of four-year-olds as they related to
the factors of racial/ethnic group membership, sex, and
degree of racial/ethnic contact in the preschool classroom. A major objective of the study was to clarify the
diversity and inconsistencies of past findings about
Black and White subjects' racial/ethnic identification
and prejudice and also to investigate the choice patterns
of Mexican-Americans. Black, White, and Mexican-American
children were shown color photos of Black, White, and
Mexican-American males and females. Results were that
White children surpassed the other groups in correct
identification. Both sexes of Black and White children
tended to identify with their own group. Mexican-American males tended to identify with the White stimulus,
while females of this group identified with their own
ethnic group. The impact of integration over segregation
improved own-group identification for Black and Mexican-
American subjects, while White subjects tended to identify more accurately in segregated settings. Additionally, preference patterns showed that the introduction
of a Mexican-American choice altered previous patterns
of White preference since both minority groups preferred
the Mexican-American stimulus over the White choice.
However, sex differences were found for this minority
response in that males preferred the White stimulus and
females preferred the Mexican-American choice.

112. St. John, N. H. "The effect of segregation on the
aspirations of Negro youth." Harvard Educational Review,
36(3), 1966, 284-294.

St. John tested the hypothesis that there was a negative
relationship between the degree of segregation and the
level of aspiration of Black students. The subject sample included all males and females (Black and White),
dropouts, and non-dropouts who were ever enrolled in the
class of 1962 in high school in a middle-sized New
England city. The results of the study did not support
the hypothesis.

113. Schenk, Q. F. and Romney, A. K. "Some differential
attitudes among adolescent groups as revealed by Bogardus'
social distance scale." Sociology and Social Research,
35(1), 1950, 38-45.

The racial attitudes of four adolescent groups, homo-
geneous as to residential area, were analyzed. The

subjects were from Gary, Indiana, a city in which Blacks
accounted for 37 percent of the population and were
forced to live in one restricted area and seldom interacted with any race other than their own. Comparisons
were made between Blacks and Whites, Whites from different sections of Gary, and different age groups within
the same area. The scale used to determine attitudes
was adapted from the original social distance measure by
Bogardus. Results, reported in Table 1 of the article,
showed that in the downtown district, Blacks, Puerto
Ricans, and Japanese received generally unfavorable
ratings. And the ratings of these subjects were statistically similar to those of the younger group from
the Glen Park area. Older subjects in the Glen Park
group tended to make fewer favorable ratings as a whole,
and Blacks again received a low rating. In contrast,
responses of subjects in the central district group,
which was made up of Blacks, placed Blacks in the highest position. All other groups, other than Blacks,
tended to receive the same number of favorable responses
from the central subjects.

114. Sciara, F. "A study of the acceptance of blackness
among Negro boys." Journal of Negro Education, 41, 1972,
151-156.

The purpose of the study was to determine if recent
efforts by society and the Black community have resulted
in greater acceptance of Blackness among Black boys than
has been indicated by previous studies. A projective
test called the Projective Picture Inventory was used.
The measure consisted of 12 cards each containing three
pictures of Black adult males making a total of 36 pictures. Each card contained a picture of a light, a
medium, and a dark male comparable in age, expression,
dress, and general appearance. Fourth-graders at a midwestern school were subjects. Subjects were asked to
select one photo on each card which he thought represented a member of the occupational group presented.
Twelve occupations were used: six of high status and
six of low status. Results showed that high-status
occupations were ascribed to light-skinned Blacks and
low-status occupations were ascribed to dark-skinned
Blacks.

115. Shaw, M. E. "The self-image of black and white pupils
in an integrated school." Journal of Personality, 42(1),
1974(Mar), 12-22.

Shaw measured the self-perceptions of Black and White
children on a self-image scale in the fall of the school
year and again in the spring. The children were from a
recently integrated school. The results showed that
males perceived themselves as less sociable, but more
independent than females; Blacks saw themselves as more
independent and hostile than Whites; sociability

increased, but achievement orientation decreased with
grade level; and Blacks in Study I decreased in sociability, but those in Study II showed no change. White students showed the reverse.

116. Solkoff, N.   "Race of experimenter as a variable in
research with children." Developmental Psychology, 7(1),
1972(Jul), 70-75.

   Four Black and four White female experimenters adminis-
   tered the WISC and Sarason's Test Anxiety Scale to Black
   and White eight- to 11-year-olds. In all cases for the
   WISC, Black students scored lower than White students.
   The race of the examiner was a significant effect on the
   Comprehension and Picture Completion subtests and on the
   Verbal, Performance, and Full Scale IQ's, of the WISC,
   with Black examiners producing the highest scores.
   There were no significant main effects or interactions
   in relation to the anxiety measure. (Summary of journal
   abstract.)

117. Stabler, J. R. and Goldberg, F. J.   "The black and white
symbolic matrix." International Journal of Symbology, 4(2),
1973(Jul), 27-35.

   Differential preference for the colors black and white
   is pervasive and develops early in life. Experiments
   with children in Louisiana and Georgia have found that
   Black and White children associate good objects with a
   white box and bad objects with a black box. In an experiment in which subjects were to guess the sound source of
   tape-recorded positive and negative self-statements, the
   children generally reported hearing positive statements
   originating from the white box and negative statements
   from the black box. Children's attitudes toward these
   two colors presumably generalize and influence their
   attitudes toward Black and White people. Studies of
   these attitudes and of ways to modify them may contrib-
   ute to an understanding of the development of racial
   attitudes. (Summary of journal abstract.)

118. Stevenson, H. W. and Stevenson, N. G.   "Social interaction in an interracial nursery school." Genetic Psychology
Monographs, 61, 1960(Feb), 37-75.

   Stevenson and Stevenson studied the social behavior of
   Black and White two- and three-year-olds at an interracial nursery school in the South. The results showed
   that most of the children were racially aware but that
   physical differences associated with race did not influence to a significant extent the type or degree of social
   interactions between the children.

119. Stevenson, H. W. and Stewart, E. C.   "A developmental
study of racial awareness in young children." Child Development, 29, 1958(Sep), 399-409.

A series of tests involving discrimination of physical
differences between Blacks and Whites and attitudes
toward race were given to Black and White students
between the ages of three and seven. It was found that
the ability to discriminate between the races increased
with age, and White children tended to develop this
ability at a younger age than Black children. Black
children made fewer own-race choices on a doll choice
test. And, Black children assigned negative roles to
Black children more often than did White children to
other Whites.

120. Stugart, D. B. "An experimental study investigating
the effects of model race and model age-referent group upon
the vocational information-seeking behaviors of male black
eleventh-graders." Dissertation Abstracts International,
31(7-A), 1971(Jan), 3281.

The purpose of the study was to examine the effects of
race and age of a model on the acquisition and performance by Black male adolescents of a model's information-
seeking behavior. It was expected that subjects who were
similar to the model in age and race would imitate him
more frequently. However, differences due to the race
and age of the model were not found. The basic conclusion was that rewarded models produced more vocationally
relevant behaviors from subjects than did models who
were not rewarded.

121. Taylor, R. G., Jr. "Racial stereotypes in young children." Journal of Psychology, 64(2), 1966, 137-142.

Taylor designed the study to learn to what extent young
children absorb commonly held negative stereotypes about
Blacks. Black and White children in grades one and three
and those whose parents had a combined income of $12,000
per year or less than $4,000 per year were used as sub-
jects. Nine photos, each showing a Black and a White
person involved in the same activity, were used as stimuli. Anecdotes implying a commonly held, negative stereotype were written to accompany the pictures. Each
child was asked to identify the person to whom the stereotype applied. The nine stereotypes were: lazy, dis-
honest, careless, unfitting as a neighbor, incompetent,
dumb, bad, and not nice. Results were that the subjects
had negative stereotypes about Blacks; that White subjects had more of these than Blacks (however, Black
children accepted the stereotypes dumb and dirty to a
high degree); controlling for race, ability, and grades,
the higher the socioeconomic status the more likely was
the child to have the stereotype; intelligence did not
affect stereotypes; and controlling for race, socioeconomic status, and ability, older children were more
likely to possess negative stereotypes than younger
children.

122. Teicher, J. D.   "Some observations on identity problems
in children of Negro-white marriages." Journal of Nervous
and Mental Disease, 146(3), 1968, 249-256.

Three case histories were done of Black children from
Black-White marriages. The findings suggested that there
tended to be resentment of both parents, an inability to
identify with either one, and resentment toward siblings
who have racial characteristics which are different.

123. Terry, R. L. and Evans, J. E.   "Class versus race discrimination attributed to self and others." Journal of Psychology, 80(2), 1972(Mar), 183-187.

The study was designed to obtain independent measures of
class and race discrimination and to determine if these
measures varied with race. It was also concerned with
whether Blacks and Whites differed in their attribution
of class and race discrimination to other people of the
same and different racial groups. Black and White high
school students from Kentucky were given questionnaires
composed of 20 descriptive statements. The subjects
were to give their endorsements of each statement as it
applied to upper classes, Blacks, lower classes, and
White individuals by checking a four-point Likert scale
concerning how these groups would respond. Results indicated that both Blacks and Whites attributed more class
discrimination to other people of either race than to
themselves. A non-significant tendency was reflected
in the endorsement X race interaction such that Blacks
and Whites tended to attribute more class discrimination
to Blacks than to Whites. And class was found to be a
more important basis for discrimination than race.

124. Vega, M. "The performance of Negro children on an
oddity discrimination task as a function of the race of the
examiner and the type of verbal incentive used by the
examiner." Dissertation Abstracts, 26, 1965, 1176-1177.

The purpose of the study was to examine the differential
effect of Black and White examiners on the performance
of southern, rural Black children on a discrimination
task. Some of the results were that sixth- and tenth-
graders of medium intelligence responded with the short-
est latency to White examiners, while those of high
intelligence responded this way to Black examiners.
And, Black examiners elicited decreased second trial
mean reaction times, while White examiners elicited
increased times.

125. Wade, K. and Wilson, W. "Relatively low prejudice in a
racially isolated group." Psychological Reports, 28, 1971,
871-877.

The study compared attitudes at two, all White, rural
high schools in Alabama with attitudes at an integrated

high school. It was hypothesized that racial isolation
would produce unfavorable attitudes toward Blacks, while
racial contact would produce favorable attitudes. The
results showed that the students at the all White schools
had more favorable attitudes. A retest at these schools
six months later showed that the attitudes had improved
significantly.

126. Ward, S. H. and Braun, J. "Self-esteem and racial preference in black children." American Journal of Orthopsychiatry, 42(4), 1972(Jul), 644-647.

The aim of the study was to examine the interrelation of
self-esteem and racial preferences in Black seven- and
eight-year-olds. It was predicted that children with
low self-esteem would be more out-group oriented than
those with high self-esteem, preferences for Whites would
be greater among middle-class than lower-class children,
and boys and girls would differ significantly in their
choice of a black or white puppet for racial preference
questions. The results supported the first prediction
but not the second or third ones. The experimenters
suggested that perhaps the middle class was just as
ethnocentric as the lower class and that males were
just as racially aware as females.

127. Washington, A. C. "Self-acceptance and group identification among a group of black upward-bound students." Dissertation Abstracts International, 31(6-B), 1970(Dec), 3695.

The aim of the study was to examine the adaptiveness of
various patterns of adjustment Blacks have made to their
marginal role in society. Second, the study was concerned with parental identification as this related to
identification by subjects with the Black in-group.
Black Upward-Bound students were subjects. One of the
results showed that there was a positive relationship
between acceptance of the same-sex parent (the mother)
and acceptance of the Black in-group among female subjects. Two other hypotheses concerning self-acceptance
and in-group reactions were not supported.

128. Webster, S. W. "The influence of interracial contact
on social acceptance in a newly integrated school." Journal
of Educational Psychology, 52(6), 1961, 292-296.

Because of the paucity of interracial contact research
concerning public schools, the study determined to study
the effects of such contact on questionnaire scores and
friendship choice in a newly integrated California junior
high school using Black and White children. Black and
White control groups from segregated schools were used.
Results showed that only Black students in the experimental group expressed more social acceptance of members
of the other race after the six-month contact period;
thus, the interracial contact did not seem to have a

significant effect. Possible explanations were suggested
by the experimenter for the disconfirmation of the contact hypothesis.

129. Webster, S. W. and Kroger, M. N. "A comparative study
of selected perceptions and feelings of Negro adolescents
with and without white friends in integrated urban high
schools." Journal of Negro Education, 35, 1966, 55-61.

The study was concerned with three types of feelings held
by Black adolescents who reported having White friends as
compared with those having no White friends. It was
found that the students with White friends had more favorable self-images and expressed higher levels of aspiration for themselves. And, students without White friends
expressed a greater preference for social interactions
with Blacks.

130. Williams, J. E. and McMurtry, C. "Color connotations
among Caucasian seventh-graders and college students." Perceptual and Motor Skills, 30(3), 1970, 707-713.

The experimenters investigated the connotative meanings
of 10 color names on 12 semantic differential scales as
rated by White seventh-grade children and college students in order to determine the degree to which the usual
adult meanings were already discernible in the responses
of the seventh-graders and the degree to which the
responses of these young subjects could be conceptualized
in terms of the three semantic dimensions. All subjects
were tested in groups in the perspective schools. The
following colors were rated: white, black, brown, yellow,
red, green, purple, orange, and gray. The results showed
that both groups of subjects rated the colors quite similarly. Analysis of the Evaluative scores for the five
race-related colors indicated that the expected positive
evaluations of white and negative evaluations of brown
and black were evident in the responses of the younger
subjects. And, the colors red and yellow were not rated
differently from the color white by the seventh-graders
as they had been by the college sample who evaluated
white less than yellow and yellow less than red.

131. Williams, J. E. and Rousseau, C. A. "Evaluation and
identification responses of Negro preschoolers to the colors
black and white." Perceptual and Motor Skills, 33(2), 1971
(Oct), 587-599.

The study was designed to assess the previously found
tendency among Black and White college students and among
White preschool children to evaluate white positively and
black negatively. It tested this response and the tendency toward self-identification with these colors using
Black preschoolers. Pictures of animals, one white and
one black, were used as stimuli. It was found that the
children associated positive adjectives with the white

figures and negative ones with the black figures. Additionally, the children tended to identify with the white figure rather than the black figure.

132. Williams, R. L. "Cognitive and affective components of southern Negro students' attitude toward academic integration." Journal of Social Psychology, 76(1), 1968, 107-111.

The study was concerned with the cognitive and affective reservations of Black high school students toward academic integration. The results showed that the students had conflict about the transition from a segregated to an integrated setting. And, while most students were philosophically committed to the change, they expressed affective concern.

133. Williams, R. L. and Venditti, F. "Effect of academic integration on southern Negro students' expressed satisfaction with school." Journal of Social Psychology, 79(2), 1969, 203-209.

At the beginning and end of the academic year 1966-1967, an opinion questionnaire was given to high school students in six racial-educational groups: Black students in newly desegregated schools, segregated schools, schools desegregated for at least one year, and White students in the same categories. The results indicated that during the year all students decreased in their satisfaction with school; Blacks expressed less satisfaction than Whites; and of the Black students, those in the segregated schools expressed the least satisfaction, and those in previously integrated schools, the greatest satisfaction. (Summary of author abstract.)

134. Williams, W. L., Jr. "A study of school desegregation: Self-prediction of behavior and correlates of self-prediction." Dissertation Abstracts, 16, 1956, 591.

The study was done in order to provide information that would help in the anticipation of problems arising in the desegregation of a school system in Tennessee. Attitudes of White students toward Black students and teachers and their perception of their parents' attitudes toward integrated schools were measured. The attitudes of Black students in this regard were determined. And, the attitudes of White teachers toward Black teachers and students were measured. It was found that there were generally favorable attitudes toward the other ethnic group by Blacks and Whites in each area.

3

RACIAL ATTITUDE CHANGE IN ADULTS

135. Banks, W. R. "Changing attitudes towards the Negro in the United States: The primary causes." Journal of Negro Education, 30, 1961, 87-93.

Banks noted that perhaps one of the most obvious elements of change in American life was attitudes toward Blacks. This change comes from three types of pressures: social, economic, and religious. The major tool of these instruments of change is education.

136. Beard, E. "The ethnic identity of the classroom instructor as a factor in changing anti-Negro attitudes of white college students." Dissertation Abstracts International, 31(3-A), 1970(Sep), 1064.

The aim of Beard's study was to examine the effects of a teacher's race on changing anti-Black attitudes among White college students. It was predicted that a Black teacher in a White classroom would effect more favorable attitude change than a White teacher in a similar situation. The two experimental groups received six lectures on the deprived Black child. The two Control Groups did not. The results were that there was no difference in the reduction of anti-Black attitudes regardless of the presence of a Black or White teacher. However, when looking at the percentage of students who shifted their attitudes in a positive, negative, or null direction, it was found that Black teachers were more effective in producing a favorable change.

137. Brown, B. S. "The effect of integrated hospital experience on the racial attitudes of schizophrenic and non-psychiatric patients." Newsletter for Research in Psychology, 6(3), 1964, 33-34.

The study was concerned with the effect of enforced racial integration over a prolonged period of time on attitudes toward Blacks by schizophrenic and non-psychiatric hospital patients. The results showed that non-psychiatric patients in contact with Blacks chose fewer Blacks on a friendship choice measure, non-psychiatric patients without contact with Blacks were

more tolerant of Blacks than non-psychiatric patients
with contact, and socioeconomic status had a significant
effect on attitudes in that low-socioeconomic patients
were more tolerant toward Blacks.   (Summary of journal
abstract.)

138. Brown, B. S. and Albee, G. W.   "The effect of integrated hospital experiences on racial attitudes: A discor-
dant note." Social Problems, 13(3), 1966, 324-333.

Brown and Albee hypothesized that White hospital patients
who had experienced desegregation would show more tolerance toward Blacks than those who had not had this experience.   Three questionnaires were administered to White
male patients between the ages of 20 and 60.   The subjects came from rural Ohio and western Pennsylvania.
The results showed that there was a significant difference between the attitudes of those who had experienced
desegregation and those who had not, but the difference
was in a direction opposite to that which had been predicted.   Patients without previous contact were more
tolerant than those with previous contact.

139. Caffrey, B., Anderson, S., and Garrison, J.   "Change in
racial attitudes of white southerners after exposure to the
atmosphere of a southern university." Psychological Reports,
25(2), 1969, 555-558.

Male and female college students were given a Likert-
type Negro Attitude Test to examine the effects of their
parents' sex, education, and time spent at the university on attitudes toward Blacks.   It was found that
seniors were less prejudiced than freshmen with male
seniors the least prejudiced; male freshmen had the
highest prejudice scores, female freshmen were next,
and female seniors next; and parental education was
not related to attitudes.

140. Carkhuff, R. R. and Banks, G.   "Training as a preferred mode of facilitating relations between races and
generations." Journal of Counseling Psychology, 17(5),
1970, 413-418.

White teachers and Black parents were divided into two
interracial groups and were systematically trained by a
Black and a White trainer in interpersonal skills.   The
aim was to effect positive changes in relations between
the two races.   The results were that after the three-
week training period there was a gain in interpersonal
skills.   Additionally, there was improvement in functioning in a helping role with Black and White adults
and children.   White teachers made more gains in reference to the adults, and Black parents made more gains
in reference to the children.

141. Carlson, E. R.   "Attitude change through modification
of attitude structure."   Journal of Abnormal and Social Psychology, 52, 1956, 256-261.

    The experiment tested the prediction that attitudes
    toward an object or situation could be changed through
    changing an individual's perception of the significance
    of the object as a means of acquiring some valued goals.
    Additionally, it investigated whether attitude change
    was generalized to other related objects and whether the
    degree of generalization depended upon the similarity of
    the objects. The subjects responded to measures of atti-
    tude toward permitting Blacks to move into White neigh-
    borhoods and other related issues, to a measure requiring
    ratings of certain values, and to a measure rating the
    probability that permitting Blacks to move into White
    neighborhoods would block the attainment of the value
    goals. It was found that among other results the per-
    ceptions of the role of Black housing segregation in
    acquiring the goals and attitudes toward housing segre-
    gation were changed. However, insufficient attitude
    change was produced in highly prejudiced and non-
    prejudiced subjects. Additionally, the extent of the
    generalization of attitude change did not vary with
    the similarity of the issue.

142. Culbertson, F. M.   "Modification of an emotionally held
attitude through role playing."   Journal of Abnormal and
Social Psychology, 54, 1957, 230-233.

    The purpose of the study was to examine (1) whether role
    playing could change an attitude, (2) whether a partici-
    pant position in a role-playing session would be more
    likely to result in attitude change than an observer
    position, and (3) whether individuals high in authori-
    tarianism were less affected by a psycho-dramatic expe-
    rience than individuals low in authoritarianism. Sub-
    jects responded to questionnaires measuring attitudes
    about permitting Blacks to move into White neighborhoods
    and general attitudes toward Blacks. The results showed
    that the subjects shifted their attitudes toward inte-
    gration in housing as well as their general attitudes
    toward Blacks. Role-playing subjects shifted to a
    greater degree than observers in a favorable direction.

143. Curto, S. E. and Sistrunk, F.   "Opinion change as a
function of the race of the experimenter, the communication
source, and the subject."   Journal of Social Psychology,
87(1), 1972(Jun), 149-150.

    The study examined the effects of race on opinion change
    in terms of Black and White experimenters, Black and
    White communicators, and Black and White subjects. Male
    high school students were given a questionnaire to deter-
    mine their opinions on various issues. Next, they were
    given printed communications presenting arguments

related to the issues and ostensibly from a professional
news service. A picture of the proposed author of the
communication was in the upper left-hand of the article.
The picture was of a Black or White person. Then, the
original opinion questionnaire was readministered. The
results showed no significant difference in questionnaire
responses after the presentation of the persuasive com-
munications.

144. Delany, L. T. "Racism and strategies for change."
Psychology Today, 2(3), 1968(Aug), 53-57.

According to Delany, "Not all Whites are racist, but most
racists are White." How can the problem of racism be
overcome? First, he says, we must understand its his-
toric roots and the numerous manifestations which this
particular and unique form of bigotry has taken. Racism
in the United States is one of the most pathological
aspects of this society. There are no simple solutions
for change. Any strategies for change must be constantly
policed to see whether they are not committing the same
mistake which created the problem.

145. Eisenman, R. "Reducing prejudice by Negro-white contacts." Journal of Negro Education, 34, 1965, 461-462.

Although the Deutsch and Collins housing study suggested
that contact between Blacks and Whites may reduce prejudice, the actual picture is more complicated. In some
instances, contact leads to an increase in prejudice
rather than a reduction. Eisenman reviewed studies for
situational and personality variables related to prejudice. He also considered the apparent inconsistency
between what people say and what they do. (Summary of
journal abstract.)

146. Greenberg, H., Pierson, J., and Sherman, S. "The
effects of single-session education techniques on prejudice
attitudes." Journal of Educational Sociology, 31, 1957,
82-86.

The purpose of the study was to test the effectiveness
of several single-session educational techniques in
changing prejudicial attitudes. Students from Texas
Technological College were subjects. The students were
given the California E Scale as a measure of prejudice.
The results showed that there was no significant change
in attitudes after the educational material had been
presented. Greenberg cautioned that although the educational manipulations were not effective, it could have
been because they were only given once.

147. Gunlach, R. H. "Effects of on-the-job experiences with
Negroes upon racial attitudes of white workers in union
shops." Psychological Reports, 2, 1956, 67-77.

Gunlach examined the racial attitudes of White working-
class women who belonged to left-wing unions toward
Blacks. He was interested in the effects of interracial, on-the-job experiences in breaking down prejudices. The results showed that there was much less
prejudice in this sample than had been previously
reported with samples from the general population and
from non-integrated and integrated housing projects.
In the present study, women who were office workers
and who came into contact with similarly educated and
cultured Blacks had the most prejudiced and hostile
feelings and were most anti-union.

148. Lagey, J. C. "Does teaching change students' attitudes." Journal of Educational Research, 50, 1956, 307-311.

Lagey tested changes in attitudes toward Blacks, toward
evaluation, and toward criminals resulting from taking
introductory courses in sociology and anthropology. He
found no relationship between course content and attitude change. Attitudes toward Blacks and evaluation did
not change significantly, and attitudes toward criminals
changed independently of the courses. (Summary of journal abstract.)

149. Pavlos, A. J. "Racial attitude and stereotype change
with bogus pipeline paradigm." Proceedings of the Annual
Convention of the American Psychological Association, 7(Pt.
1), 1972, 291-292.

Three different levels of discrepant bogus physiological
feedbacks were given to male and female undergraduates
showing that their racial attitudes were not as negative
as they had predicted. Half of the subjects filled out
a self-report dependent measure, and the remaining subjects were put through a bogus pipeline paradigm dependent measure. Subjects' racial stereotypes were then
measured to check for predicted corresponding stereotype
changes. The results showed that significantly greater
attitude change occurred only with the highest level of
discrepant feedback and only when measured by the bogus
pipeline paradigm. Additionally, subjects showing a
significant racial attitude change also showed a significant racial stereotype change. (Summary of author
abstract.)

150. Rhyne, D. C. "Attitude set, group learning, and attitude change." Dissertation Abstracts, 29(4-A), 1968, 1098-
1099.

The aim of the study was to determine the degree of
attitude change related to attitude set; group learning
method; and race, age, and sex. A secondary aim was to
evaluate the effectiveness of an intensive adult education program in changing the degree of prejudice in
various dimensions. One of the findings were that the

degree of attitude change in the direction of tolerance
as related to participation in the program was greater
on the rational-irrational anti-minority dimension of
prejudice among participants with high and medium social
attitude sets and among those who were 41 years old and
older.

151. Rosen, B. "Attitude change within the Negro press
toward segregation and discrimination." Journal of Social
Psychology, 62(1), 1964, 77-83.

Rosen examined the change in attitude among Blacks
toward militancy and gradualism and whether the change
was reflected in the Black middle-class press. Ebony
magazine was used as a source. A significant difference was found between the way articles on discrimination were presented in 1948 and 1960. Articles published in 1960 tended to be more direct and made
discrimination an important aspect of the article.
Additionally, in 1948 a majority of the articles men-
tioned Whites, while in 1960 the articles were divided
evenly between the two races. Other results were also
discussed.

152. Rubin, I. "The reduction of prejudice through labora-
tory training." Journal of Applied Behavioral Science,
3(1), 1967, 29-50.

The study tested the hypothesis that increases in self-
acceptance resulting from sensitivity training would
reduce an individual's level of prejudice. Black and
White males and females ranging in age from 23 to 59
were subjects. It was found that sensitivity training
may be a powerful technique to be used in the reduction
of prejudice, especially with those who are low in psychological anomie or a sense of normlessness.

153. Saylor, R. I. "An exploration of race prejudice in
college students and interracial contact." Dissertation
Abstracts International, 30(6-A), 1969, 2620.

The aim of the study was to investigate the effects of
various types of interracial contact on attitudes of
race prejudice in Whites using White college students
and Black pre-college students in a tutorial situation
as subjects. The Multifactor Racial Attitude Inventory
and the Dogmatism Scale were used. Results showed that
age and college class status were not significantly
related to attitudes of race prejudice according to
the Multifactor Racial Attitude Inventory responses,
males were less prejudiced than females, non-church
attenders were less prejudiced than church attenders,
dogmatism was related to prejudice, and individuals
exposed to interracial contact in the tutoring situation were less prejudiced than those not exposed.

154. Young, R. K., Benson, W. M., and Holtzman, W. H.
"Change in attitudes toward the Negro in a southern univer-
sity." <u>Journal of Abnormal and Social Psychology</u>, 60, 1960
(Jan), 131-133.

    Young et al. were interested in determining whether there
    existed a change in attitudes toward Blacks at the Univer-
    sity of Texas three years after an earlier survey had
    been taken. The results showed that attitudes toward
    Blacks were very stable. However, women were somewhat
    more tolerant in 1958 than in 1955, while the attitude
    of men was in the reverse direction.

4

CONCOMITANTS OF RACIAL ATTITUDES

155. Allport, G. W. "Prejudice: Is it societal or personal?" Religious Education, 59(1), 1964, 20-29.

Allport noted that some social scientists were asserting that there was too much emphasis upon investigating the effects of personality on prejudice. They suggested that the true dynamics of racial and ethnic relationships could be better understood through group phenomena and that social scientists should take a societal approach to the study of prejudice. Allport presented both arguments: the societal and the personality approach. He concluded that there was no reason for rivalry among social scientists preferring one approach over the other. They should and could blend the two.

156. Bayton, J. A., McAllister, L. B., and Hamer, J. "Race-class stereotypes." Journal of Negro Education, 25, 1956, 75-78.

The study investigated racial stereotypes in terms of class within race. It was hypothesized that racial stereotypes would vary according to class designations within the races being stereotyped. White and Black college students were subjects. The White subjects came from a border state university with few Blacks enrolled, and the Black subjects attended a virtually all Black university. Subjects were asked to select from a list of 85 adjectives any which they felt described each of the following: upper-class White Americans, upper-class Blacks, lower-class Whites, and lower-class Blacks. After choosing as many adjectives per group as they felt were descriptive, they starred the five which they considered to be most typical of the group. These groups of five were the basis for the stereotypes. Results showed that stereotypes varied more as a function of class than race. For example, White and Black subjects described both upper-class Whites and Blacks as intelligent, ambitious, industrious, neat, and progressive, while lower-class Whites and Blacks were described as ignorant, lazy, loud, and physically dirty. The items assigned to both classes of Whites by White subjects were materialistic and pleasure-loving. Black subjects

assigned the adjective tradition-loving to Whites. Both
classes of Blacks were described as musical and ostentatious by White subjects, but there was no item assigned
to both classes of Blacks by Black subjects.

157. Bayton, J. A. and Muldrow, T. W. "Interacting variables in the perception of racial personality traits."
Journal of Experimental Research in Personality, 3(1), 1968,
39-44.

Black college students were given a survey which asked
how they thought very light-skinned Blacks and very dark-
skinned Blacks would answer the items. The sex and self-
judgments of the subjects' own skin color were used in
the analysis. Attributes of the subjects interacted
with cues concerning "the observed" in determining personality assessments. Differentiation of observer attributes seemed to be related to determination of the traits
of "the observed." Light-skinned Black males seemed to
have some difficulties in their self-concept vis-à-vis
dark-skinned Blacks. (Summary of journal abstract.)

158. Bloom, P. S. "A study of the response styles of high
dogmatic and low dogmatic low-prejudice white people in an
interpersonal situation with poor black people." Dissertation Abstracts International, 31(12-B), 1971(Jun), 7588.

The study investigated the responses of high-, middle-,
and low-dogmatic subjects in a simulated interpersonal
situation with a poor Black person and a poor White person. College students were subjects. The subjects lis-
tened to two conversations supposedly between a worker
in a social center and individuals who came to the center (one Black, one White). Subjects were to imagine
that they were the worker and responded to the individuals by speaking into a tape recorder at certain intervals in the conversations. The subjects also filled out
questionnaires concerning their impressions of the two
female persons. The results were that there was no significant difference between the three dogmatism groups
in regard to verbal and questionnaire responses. The
subjects responded similarly to the two poor people when
they were Black, but differently when they were White.

159. Brown, B. S. "A comparison of schizophrenic and normal
attitudes on the issue of race." Proceedings of the 73rd
Annual Convention of the American Psychological Association,
1965, 195-196.

Normal and mental patient White male adults were given a
Bogardus Scale which measured attitudes toward Blacks in
the hospital and a Desegregation Scale which measured
attitudes toward Blacks in general. The results were
that there were no significant differences between the
responses of the normal and mental hospital groups.

160. Burnham, K. E., Connors, J. F., III, and Leonard, R. C. "Racial prejudice in relation to education, sex, and religion." Journal for the Scientific Study of Religion, 8(2), 1969(Fal), 318.

The experimenters studied White college students from four colleges in metropolitan Philadelphia. Their findings confirmed previous results of the relationship between prejudice, sex, socioeconomic level, and religious affiliation. Students whose fathers were college graduates were low in prejudice. This relationship was nonexistent among Catholic students, small for those of no religion, great for Protestants, and particularly large among Jews. Women were low in prejudice; however, this sex difference lessened with education controlled. Finally, Catholic students were less likely to be low prejudiced, and those with no religion were more likely to be low prejudiced as compared with the others.

161. Burnstein, E. and McRae, A. V. "Some effects of shared threat and prejudice in racially mixed groups." Journal of Abnormal and Social Psychology, 64(4), 1962, 257-263.

The aim of the study was to examine the relationship between shared threat and the expression of prejudice. State college students were categorized according to anti-Black prejudice and were put under conditions of shared threat or non-threat in task-oriented cooperative work groups. A Black male confederate was a member of each group. The results were that under conditions of shared threat a decrease in expressed prejudice occurred in terms of direct evaluation of the confederate by group members on a posttask questionnaire. Additionally, significantly fewer messages were sent to the confederate by highly prejudiced students, regardless of the threat condition.

162. Buys, C. J. and Bebeau, C. E. "Prejudice, socioeconomic status, and public attitudes toward riots and demonstrations." Psychological Reports, 29(2), 1971(Oct), 451-458.

The experimenters studied perceptions of threat, causes, and treatment of racial riots and demonstrations in relation to sociological and psychological variables. A sample survey of a community in Colorado was made. The results showed that socioeconomic status and prejudice were good predictors of perceptions of the above variables. High socioeconomic status was associated with more tolerant attitudes toward these disturbances, and high prejudice was associated with less tolerant attitudes.

163. Capel, W. C. "Cognitive dissonance, reconstruction and civil rights: Applications of a theory." Journal of Human Relations, 19(2), 1971, 225-238.

Capel applied the theory of cognitive dissonance to the
events of Reconstruction in North and South Carolina.
He suggested that the failure of the movement begun by
Reconstruction to extend civil rights to Blacks could
be explained in part by the failure of the measures to
create a degree of dissonance whose reduction would have
created a change in attitude toward these rights on the
part of Whites. He suggested that the occasion arose
again in 1954 and that the opportunity also failed at
that time. He discussed the nature of the failure from
the standpoint that cognitive dissonance might be used
to bring about attitude change in situations involving
deep-seated prejudices.

164. Cole, S., Steinberg, J., and Burkheimer, G. J. "Prejudice and conservatism in a recently integrated southern
college." Psychological Reports, 23(1), 1968, 149-150.

Cole et al. wanted to determine whether token integration in a southern school improved the racial feelings
of White students toward Black students. The results
seemed to show that the White students remained highly
prejudiced. The experimenters concluded that passive
noninvolved contact between the races does not reduce
prejudice.

165. Delk, J. L. "Prejudice, perception, and penal judgments." Dissertation Abstracts, 28(7-B), 1968, 3059.

The study investigated prejudice and its effects on perception and penal judgments. Black and White college
students were chosen on the basis of scores on a prejudice scale. The subjects were to match the color on a
color mixer, which served as background for certain cut-
out figures, with the color of the gray figure. No significant differences were found, even for the matching
of the White representative and Black representative
profile cut-outs. Next, subjects took the role of crim-
inal court judges and were to pass sentence on a Black
or White defendant found guilty of armed robbery. The
results were that the students imposed significantly
longer sentences on the White defendant than on the
Black one.

166. Deslonde, J. L., III. "Beliefs in internal-external
control of reinforcements, racial ideology, and militancy
of urban community college students." Dissertation Abstracts
International, 32(1-A), 1971(Jul), 234.

The purpose of the study was to examine the relationship
between racially militant beliefs among Black college
students and their beliefs about control over their
environment. The responses of Black and White students
were examined. The findings indicated that levels of
beliefs in personal control did not influence differences between Black and White subjects' beliefs in race

ideology. Additionally, belief in external control (an
orientation held more by Black students than White students) of reinforcements and externality in race ideology influenced Black students' approval of racially
militant groups and techniques but not their relationships with campus organizations.

167. Dizard, J. E.   "Black identity, social class, and black
power."   Psychiatry, Washington, D.C., 33(2), 1970(May),
195-207.

Dizard examined Black identity or group consciousness
and current manifestations of the phenomenon in the
Black community. Black residents of Berkeley, California, were interviewed in 1967 on a number of attitudes and experiences. It was found that high attachment to Black identity was higher among younger and
better educated Blacks. Lowest attachment was found
among such individuals as proprietors-managers, service
workers, and craftsmen. These groups were also found
to be lower in militancy. Dizard predicted an increase
in Black identity and pride and a growing sharpness in
the conflict between Blacks and Whites. (Summary of
journal abstract.)

168. Eisenman, R. and Cole, S. N.   "Prejudice and conservatism in denominational college students."   Psychological
Reports, 14(2), 1964, 644.

Nine male and two female students at a southern college
who were affiliated with the Baptist religion were subjects. The senior author collected the opinions
expressed by these students about the race issue during
their class meetings. Twenty conservative and no liberal statements were made. Therefore, the findings suggested that there was a positive relationship between
religion and prejudice.

169. Epstein, R. and Baron, R. M.   Cognitive dissonance and
projected hostility toward out-groups."   Journal of Social
Psychology, 79(2), 1969, 171-182.

Epstein and Baron tested the theory of cognitive dissonance which predicts that strong confrontation with
hostile impulses will lead high self-esteem subjects
to project these impulses toward Whites and that denial
of hostile impulses is related to projection toward
Blacks. The results indicated that the denial of hostility facilitated the attribution of negative qualities
toward Blacks. (Summary of author abstract.)

170. Erb, D. L.   "Racial attitudes and empathy: A Guttman
facet theory examination of their relationships and determinants."   Dissertation Abstracts International, 30(12-A),
1970(Jun), 5234.

The aim of the study was to test Allport's theory that empathy and prejudice were inversely related and to study the relationship between prejudice personal contact, change orientation, religiosity, and efficacy. White college seniors were subjects. The results showed that the predicted relationship between prejudice and empathy was not supported. The relationship between contact and prejudice was supported with enjoyment of, nature of, and amount of contact with Blacks being the most significant contributors to this variable. The relationships between change orientation and prejudice and efficacy and prejudice were supported; however, the relationship between religiosity and prejudice was not supported.

171. Feagin, J. R. "Prejudice and religious types: A focused study of southern fundamentalists. Journal for the Scientific Study of Religion, 4(1), 1964, 3-13.

The study was done in order to test the relationship between prejudice and religiosity. Questionnaires were administered to the members of five Baptist churches in four cities in two southern border states. Some of the findings were that church members who were less devote in their religion were more prejudiced than those who were more devote. And, the more orthodox the church member, the more prejudiced he was likely to be.

172. Frankel, S. A. and Barrett, J. "Variations in personal space as a function of authoritarianism, self-esteem, and racial characteristics of a stimulus situation." Journal of Consulting and Clinical Psychology, 37(1), 1971, 95-98.

The objectives of the study were to investigate the effects of presentations of Black and White human stimuli on personal space and to study the relationship between personal space, authoritarianism, and self-esteem. White male undergraduates were subjects. Two male college students, one White and one Black, were stimuli. It was predicted that when approached by White and Black stimuli the largest area of personal space would be used by subjects high in authoritarianism and low in self-esteem and that these subjects would also use larger areas of personal space in response to the approach of the Black stimulus than the White stimulus. Results showed that low self-esteem subjects used greater personal space distances in response to the Black stimulus than to the White stimulus. High authoritarian subjects used larger areas of space in response to the Black stimulus than to the White stimulus. The significant race X self-esteem X authoritarian interaction showed that greater personal space was used by high authoritarian, low self-esteem subjects toward the Black stimulus. Lastly, low authoritarian subjects showed a similar response toward the stimulus, while high authoritarian and self-esteem subjects used smaller areas than did high authoritarian, low self-esteem subjects.

173. Frazier, E. F.   "The Negro middle class and desegregation." Social Problems, 4, 1957, 291-301.

Middle-class Blacks conform more readily to the American
standards of behavior than any other element in the
Black population. This group is comprised almost
entirely of white-collar workers. Desegregation threat-
ens their high prestige and status in the Black community; consequently, at times it seems that they have
acquired a vested interest in segregation. The Black
community will only "wither away" slowly and only as
desegregation proceeds to progress. As greater oppor-
tunities are given Blacks of the middle class, they will
acquire new responsibilities which will speed up desegregation. (Summary of journal abstract.)

174. Green, J.   "Attitudinal and situational determinants of
intended behavior towards Negroes." Dissertation Abstracts,
28(9-A), 1968, 3767-3768.

Green was concerned with the relationship of attitude,
level of anticipated disapproval, degree of intimacy of
an anticipated relationship, and socioeconomic-educa-
tional level of an anticipated Black associate. The
results showed that attitude and degree of intimacy of
an anticipated relationship were strong determinants of
readiness to pose in interracial scenes (the dependent
variable). Moderately anti-Black subjects were more
unwilling to pose in interracial pictures than moderately equalitarian subjects. Additionally, as the
degree of intimacy of an anticipated relationship
increased, unwillingness to pose in the photos
increased.

175. Greenfield, R. W.   "Factors associated with attitudes
toward desegregation in a Florida residential suburb."
Social Forces, 40, 1961, 31-42.

Greenfield investigated the distribution of attitudes
of White parents of school children in a culturally
heterogeneous southern population and the characteristics of respondents who are in favor of or opposed to
desegregation. He found that the attitudes of the parents varied widely but were predominantly unfavorable.
Furthermore, favorable and unfavorable attitudes were
significantly related to occupational prestige, education, exposure to southern race relation norms, and to
regional self-identification.

176. Greenfield, R. W.   "Factors associated with white parents' attitudes toward school desegregation in a central
Florida community." Dissertation Abstracts, 20, 1960(Mar),
3871-3872.

Greenfield hypothesized that attitudes toward school
desegregation among White parents in Florida would be

predominantly unfavorable, but those who were pro-
desegregation would be characterized by a higher level of
education, a high prestige occupation, being born in the
North, living only a short time in the South, and being
relatively young. The analysis tended to support these
relationships, but with some qualifications. For example, while those favoring desegregation tended to be of
relatively high educational achievement, there was
almost an even distribution of college-educated parents
among those who were favorable toward desegregation and
those who were not.

177. Haggstrom, W. C. "Self-esteem and other characteristics of residentally desegregated Negroes." Dissertation
Abstracts, 23(8), 1963, 3007-3008.

The purpose of the study was to test the hypothesis that
the Black community is a symbol of Black inferiority and
depresses the self-esteem of its members. From this it
was predicted that the level of self-esteem of members
of a residentially segregated area would be higher than
that of members of a segregated area. The results
showed that members of desegregated areas had higher
self-esteem than those of segregated areas.

178. Hites, R. W. and Kellogg, E. P. "The F and social
maturity scales in relation to racial attitudes in a deep
south sample." Journal of Social Psychology, 62(2), 1964,
189-195.

Hites and Kellogg tested the relationship between authoritarianism, personality, and prejudice among freshmen in
a Deep South college. The tests given to the students
were the F Scale, which is a measure of authoritarianism;
the Social Maturity Scale, which measured personality;
and two items concerning segregation. The results showed
that individuals who were highly authoritarian or who
were socially mature tended to be more likely to agree
with segregation, and those who were less authoritarian
or socially mature were against segregation. However,
some students, both high F Scale and Social Maturity
Scale scores, were for integration, and some with low
scores on these measures were for segregation.

179. Katz, I. and Benjamin, L. "Effects of white authoritarianism in biracial work groups." Journal of Abnormal and
Social Psychology, 61(3), 1960, 448-456.

Black and White male college students worked in groups
of four--two Black and two White--on a series of tasks.
Some of the results showed that when a task required
close cooperation between two subjects, White authoritarians accepted significantly more suggestions from
Blacks. On tasks requiring group decisions, White
authoritarians were more compliant and White authoritarians rated Blacks as more intelligent, mature, and

dominant. Finally, Blacks who worked with White authoritarians were generally more assertive and cooperative
than those who worked with nonauthoritarians.

180. Katz, I. and Cohen, M. "The effects of training Negroes
upon cooperative problem solving in biracial teams." Journal
of Abnormal and Social Psychology, 64(5), 1962, 319-325.

Dyads composed of Black and White male northern college
students engaged in cooperative problem solving. Unknown
to the students, each received different information so
that only one could solve any particular problem. Under
Assertion Training, the member with the easy version was
able to give the correct answer with confidence. Under
No Training, the person with the easy version was not
forced to give the correct answer. The results were that
the influence of the Black student increased in Assertion
Training and decreased in No Training. Also, the relationship between movement of the Black student's private
judgments toward the partner's judgments and the partner's previous accuracy increased in Assertion Training.

181. Killian, L. M. and Haer, T. L. "Variables related to
attitudes regarding school desegregation among white southerners." Sociometry, 21, 1958, 159-164.

A representative sample of the White adult population of
Tallahassee, Florida, was asked the degree to which they
accepted or rejected the Supreme Court's decision of
May, 1954. Acceptors in contrast to resisters had the
following characteristics: they were young, had a college or postgraduate education, held professional or
managerial positions, and lived less than half their
lives in the South; they respected the law, did not
ascribe the personal or cultural inferiority of Blacks
to inherent, racial characteristics; they were willing
to accept equal status contacts with Blacks in a variety of situations; and they were accurately informed of
the legal sanctions which could be applied by federal
judges if their orders were defied. (Summary of journal abstract.)

182. Kirkhart, R. O. "Psychological and social-psychologi-
cal correlates of marginality in Negroes." Dissertation
Abstracts, 20, 1960(Apr), 4173.

The purpose of the study was to investigate the nature
of Black people's reaction to minority group status and
to explore the relationships between this reaction and
several other variables: leadership choice, prejudice
toward other minorities, belief in internal versus
external locus of control, status striving, gradations
of skin color, music preferences, and religious affiliation. Some of the results showed that those who identified with being Black were chosen as leaders most
often, were not particularly low in prejudice toward

other minorities, were not significantly different from
those who did not identify in terms of music preference,
and had darker skin than the other group.

183. Kirtley, D. "Conformity and prejudice in authoritarians of opposing political ideologies." Journal of Psychology, 70(2), 1968, 199-204.

The aim of the study was to determine the relationships
between authoritarianism; political ideology; prejudice
toward Blacks, Puerto Ricans, Chinese, Hindus, and Bud-
dhists; and conformity under social pressure. Male college students were subjects. Some of the results were
that authoritarian subjects were more likely to yield to
pressures for increased prejudice than for decreased
prejudice and similar patterns of conformity and prejudice were found for all authoritarians whether they were
leftists, moderates, or rightists.

184. Lewis, D. G. "A study of the motivational basis of
anti-Negro prejudice in a southern sample." Dissertation
Abstracts, 23(1), 1962, 338.

The four hypotheses tested by Lewis were: (1) White
college students' prejudice toward Blacks would not be
associated with severity and domination in their parents' child-rearing practices, (2) there would be a
greater relationship between parent-offspring attitudes
toward Blacks in the South than in the North and in the
South this relationship would be greater than for more
general ethnocentrism, (3) southern subjects would not
exceed northern subjects in ethnocentrism and authoritarianism, and (4) prejudice toward Blacks would be
more related to ethnocentrism and authoritarianism in
the North than South. None of these hypotheses was
confirmed.

185. Littig, L. W. "Negro personality correlates of aspiration to traditionally open and closed occupations." Journal of Negro Education, 37(1), 1968, 31-36.

Littig assessed the relationship between achievement
motivation, social class, and aspirations to traditionally open and traditionally closed occupations among
male, Black college students. He found that high
achievement motivation and membership in the working
class were related to aspirations to traditionally
closed jobs. Low achievement motivation and middle-
class membership were associated with aspirations to
traditionally closed jobs.

186. Liu, W. T. "The community reference system, religiosity, and race attitudes." Social Forces, 39, 1961, 324-328.

Liu analyzed the attitudes of a group of Catholics who
migrated from other regions (particularly the North) to

Tallahassee, Florida. The attitudes were measured during racial tensions concerning a bus boycott incident in
1957. White married couples were subjects and were
interviewed. The results suggested that moral values
did not determine the individual's attitudes toward
desegregation. Residential stability and identification
with the southern community appeared to be the most
important factors.

187. Luchterhand, E. and Weller, L. "Social class and the
desegregation movement: A study of parents' decisions in a
Negro ghetto." Social Problems, 13(1), 1965, 83-88.

The study was concerned with the social class level of
Black parents who keep their children in a segregated
elementary school or transfer them. It was also concerned with the relationship of the demographic characteristics of the parents, the decision-making process,
and organizational membership to parental decisions.
Black families were interviewed by Black interviewers.
The results showed that more transfers (to segregated
schools) were made by low-socioeconomic families, and
mothers in the transfer group had less education than
those in the group who remained. More transfers than
remainers belonged to the National Association for the
Advancement of Colored People and the Urban League.
And, more showed agreement between spouses.

188. Maranell, G. M. "An examination of some religious and
political attitude correlates of bigotry." Social Forces,
45(3), 1967, 356-362.

Maranell reported an investigation of the religious and
political attitude correlates of bigotry. Bigotry was
defined as anti-Semitism and anti-Black attitudes.
College students from four universities were subjects:
in a midwestern rural area, a midwestern urban area, a
southern rural area, and a southern urban area. It was
found that political conservatism was highly correlated
with bigotry, and only certain aspects of religiosity
were related to bigotry, except in the southern urban
population where there was a more general significant
positive correlation between bigotry and religiosity.

189. Noel, D. I. and Pinkney, A. "Correlates of prejudice:
Some racial differences and similarities." American Journal
of Sociology, 69(6), 1964, 609-622.

Data from White and Black residents of four American
cities were analyzed in order to determine racial differences and similarities in the correlates of racial
prejudice. The cities covered were in California, New
York, Georgia, and Ohio. A social-distance scale was
used as the measure of prejudice. It was found that
there was no difference between Blacks and Whites in
terms of the relationship between prejudice and

education, age, sex, marital status, interracial contact, and authoritarianism. However, occupational status and social participation were negatively related to
anti-Black prejudice, but not significantly related to
anti-White prejudice.

190. Parker, S. and Kleiner, R. "Status position, mobility,
and ethnic identification of the Negro." Journal of Social
Issues, 20, 1964, 85-102.

The purpose of the study was to investigate the relationship between ethnic identification and status position
and also between identification and mobility. The data
for the present article were collected as part of a
larger project on the relationship between mental illness and the discrepancy between aspiration and achievement. Two subject samples were tested--a psychiatric
sample and members of a Black community in Philadelphia.
Subjects were from 20 to 60 years old. The attitude
instrument was a questionnaire, and interviews were conducted by Blacks approximately the same age as the subjects. Only results concerning ethnic attitudes and
identification will be reported. To hypothetical situations concerning how they would feel if they heard
various favorable or unfavorable new reports about
Blacks, more upper- than lower-status subjects denied
their involvement in the latter situation by expressing
that they would not feel very or fairly uncomfortable
about the report. However, they expressed that they
would be proud and enthusiastic about the successful
report. To a question regarding reactions to a friend's
intention to pass for White, the number of subjects who
expressed that they would be angry decreased as status
rose. In general, Blacks in the higher positions were
found to have values more similar to those of the White
middle class, stronger desires to associate with Whites,
more negative attitudes toward other Blacks, and a relatively weaker ethnic identification than lower-status
subjects.

191. Pavlak, T. J. "Social class, ethnicity, and racial
prejudice." Public Opinion Quarterly, 37(2), 1973(Sum),
225-231.

Pavlak tested the relationship between ethnicity, social
status, and racial prejudice. Interviews were conducted
among a sample of five major ethnic groups in a predominantly working and lower-middle-class community in
Chicago during the spring and summer of 1969. The
results showed that Polish-American and Lithuanian-
American subjects were most likely to object to having
Blacks as neighbors, while Czechoslovak-American subjects were least likely to object. However, despite
the differences in cultural background, recentness of
immigration, and experiences in American society, there
was a striking similarity among the racial attitudes of
the respondents.

192. Pettigrew, T. F. "Personality and sociocultural factors in inter-group attitudes: A cross-national comparison." Conflict Resolution II, 1, 1958(Mar), 29-42.

The paper summarized research designed to gain cross-
national perspectives on two prejudice factors--person-
ality and cultural norms. The two samples studied were
the Union of South Africa and the Southern United States
with comparisons made between the two.

193. Pettigrew, T. F. "Regional differences in anti-Negro
prejudice." Journal of Abnormal and Social Psychology, 59
(1), 1959(Jul), 28-36.

The study tested the basic hypothesis that anti-Black
prejudice among White adults in the South was "more
related to socio-cultural and social adjustment factors
and less related to externalizing personality factors
than in the North (p. 28)." Among the results from
interviews was the fact that there was more anti-Black
prejudice in the southern sample than the northern group.
And sex effects showed that southern females were more
prejudiced than men, but that there were no sex differences in the northern sample. Further analysis on the
data included an examination of the effects of military
service, political party, church attendance, and social
mobility on authoritarianism, anti-Semitism, and anti-
Black prejudice.

194. Prothro, E. T. and Jensen, J. A. "Interrelations of
religious and ethnic attitudes in selected southern populations." Journal of Social Psychology, 32, 1950, 45-49.

The experimenters attempted to determine the degree of
relationship between attitudes toward Jews, Blacks, and
the Church in six southern colleges. Catholic and Protestant college students were subjects. Questionnaires
were administered during regular class time. Part I of
the questionnaire contained a personal data sheet concerning age, sex, religious affiliation, birthplace, residence, and father's occupation. Parts II and III were
Forms A and B of the Grice-Remmers Generalized Scales.
Half of the subjects were given Form A pertaining to
Blacks and Form B pertaining to Jews; the other half were
given Form A for Jews and Form B for Blacks. Part IV of
the questionnaire was the Thurstone-Clave Scale for measuring attitudes toward the church. Results indicated
that more positive attitudes were held toward Jews than
toward Blacks. A slightly significant relationship was
found between attitudes toward the church and attitudes
toward the two ethnic groups such that favorable attitudes toward the church were correlated with favorable
attitudes toward Blacks and Jews.

195. Roberts, A. H. and Rokeach, M. "Anomie, authoritarianism, and prejudice: A replication." American Journal of
Sociology, 61, 1956, 355-358.

The study was done in order to replicate Srole's study
of the relationship between anomie, authoritarianism,
and prejudice. White, non-Jewish adult Americans were
interviewed in their homes. It was found that both
authoritarianism and anomie were related to prejudice.
In disagreement with Srole, Roberts found that both
authoritarianism and anomie were related independently
to prejudice, and anomie, as measured, was not a function of status.

196. Robin, S. S. and Story, F. "Ideological consistency of
college students: The bill of rights and attitudes towards
minority groups." Sociology and Social Research, 48(2),
1964, 187-196.

The research questioned the association of belief in the
bill of rights and attitudes toward minority groups among
individuals not necessarily bound to such informal statements of ideology. College students were subjects.
Agreement with the bill of rights was measured on a
Likert scale of 15 items. Racial attitudes were determined by an Attitudes Toward Minority Group Scale which
was also a Likert-type scale. In general, the entire
subject sample was in agreement with the bill and
accepting of minority groups including Blacks, Jews,
Spanish-Americans, American-Indians, Italian-Americans,
Chinese-Americans, Japanese-Americans, Russian-Americans,
and those generally thought of as being non-White. The
correlation between the two variables was .43, a moderate relationship. The correlation by sex was .47 for
males and .35 for females. By grade level, the correlation was .34 for freshmen, .50 for sophomores, and .70
for juniors; however, seniors had a correlation of .22
(an unexpected finding). By college, correlations were
.55 for those enrolled in the college of arts and science, .51 and .49 for agriculture and forestry, respectively. None of the correlations for those in the colleges of Engineering, Veterinary Medicine, and Home
Economics were significant. By social faternal organizations, the correlations were .44 for nonmembers and
.27 for members.

197. Rubin-Rabson, G. "Liberalism toward Negroes as a
deviant reaction in a conservative group." Journal of
Social Psychology, 41, 1955, 139-148.

The author found that a group of adults, somewhat above
average in schooling and intelligence, did not conform
with accepted prejudice patterns, but comprised a new
one: religious and political-economic conservatives
with liberal attitudes toward Blacks. It was suggested
that this finding could be due to the emphasis on inter-
cultural relations programs in the school and to the
fact that the subjects who were of the white-collar
business and professional group had little contact with

Blacks and no competition in social or work areas. However, the status of Blacks in the city of Fort Wayne, Indiana (the area studied by the experimenter), bore little relationship to these liberal attitudes. Consequently, the experimenter concluded that the question arose whether any verbal racial attitude measure could adequately catch the nuances of the deeper affect on which behavior depends.

198. Schaffer, R. C. and Schaffer, A. "Socialization and the development of attitudes toward Negroes in Alabama." Phylon, 27(3), 1966, 274-285.

Sociology students at an Alabama university gave anonymous life histories concerning their attitudes toward Blacks, why they held these attitudes, and some demographic information about their home communities. It was determined that most important in shaping attitudes was the method and content of socialization used by parents. Additionally, 34 percent of the students were classified as equalitarians, 47 percent as semi-equalitarian, and 19 percent as anti-equalitarian. (Summary of journal abstract.)

199. Shannon, B. E. "The impact of racism on personality development." Social Casework, 54(9), 1973(Nov), 519-525.

Shannon pointed out that the development of increased diagnostic awareness and sensitivity in regard to Black clients is important in the social work profession. This may be accomplished by attempting to understand the unique situation Blacks find themselves in due to continual victimization by racist strategies.

200. Silverman, I. and Kleinman, D. "A response deviance interpretation of the effects of experimentally induced frustration on prejudice." Journal of Experimental Research in Personality, 2(2), 1967, 150-153.

Frustrated and non-frustrated female college students were measured on racial prejudice and the tendency to respond in a socially deviant way on attitude scales unrelated to prejudice. It was found that frustrated students scored higher on the prejudice scales and on all measures of response deviance.

201. Simon, W. B. "Race relations and class structures." Journal of Social Psychology, 60(2), 1963, 187-193.

Simon discussed the issue of anti-Black attitudes among lower-class southern Whites. He also presented an interpretation of the interrelationships between family structure, personality, and political attitudes and their affects on Black and White racial attitudes.

202. Smith, E. W. and Dixon, T. R. "Verbal conditioning as a
function of race of the experimenter and prejudice of the
subject." Journal of Experimental Social Psychology, 4(3),
1968, 285-301.

The study tested whether a White female subject's prejudice toward Blacks would render a Black experimenter less
effective than a White experimenter in a verbal conditioning task. To condition the subjects, each received
a verbal reinforcement ("good") every time he chose a
first-person subject pronoun to begin a sentence. Smith
and Dixon found that conditioning occurred with prejudiced subjects more than with non-prejudiced subjects
and that prejudiced subjects conditioned with the White
experimenters, but not with the Black experimenters.

203. Steckler, G. A. "Authoritarian ideology in Negro college students." Journal of Abnormal and Social Psychology,
54, 1957, 396-399.

The purpose of the study was to investigate authoritarian
ideologies in Blacks. Questionnaires were administered
to a large sample of Black students enrolled at predominantly Black colleges. Some of the results showed that
there was a tendency for the students to disagree with
ethnocentric and anti-White ideologies, but to agree
with authoritarian, anti-Black, and conservative ideologies. Steckler interpreted the results as indicating
an attempt by Black middle-class students to identify
with stereotyped White middle-class values and to dis-
sociate themselves from Blacks.

204. Stevenson, M. A. and Ferguson, L. W. "The effects on
personality-impression formation of the cold-warm dimension,
the frown-smile dimension, and the Negro-white dimension."
Psychological Record, 18(2), 1968, 215-224.

Subjects were required to respond to one or more of four
portraits (a frowning Black or White person, and a smil-
ing Black or White person) by checking which trait in
each of 18 pairs of bipolar traits was more characteristic of the person portrayed. The importance of the
cold-warm dimension on personality impression formation
was verified. And, it was also discovered that a frown-
smile dimension had significant gestalt-like effects.
(Summary of journal abstract.)

205. Stotland, E. and Patchen, M. "Identification and
changes in prejudice and in authoritarianism." Journal of
Abnormal and Social Psychology, 62(2), 1961, 265-274.

The purpose of the study was to test the claim that a
person's level of prejudice could be reduced by communi-
cating to him the irrational, emotional bases of this
attitude. The assumption was that, because people feel
that irrationality and emotionality are bad, they should

look negatively upon anyone with these attributes.
Female college students at a midwestern university were
subjects. Results were contrary to the prediction and
showed that for individuals of little prejudice there
was a tendency to become more prejudiced when they found
that they had characteristics in common with a highly
prejudiced person. And, individuals who were initially
prejudiced did not change.

206. Torrence, L. A. "A study of factors associated with
Negro teachers' attitudes and opinions toward faculty desegregation." Dissertation Abstracts International, 30(7-A),
1970, 2863-2864.

The aim of the study was to determine the attitudes and
opinions concerning faculty desegregation held by Black
public school teachers in Arkansas. Some of the results
of the study showed that Black teachers wanted faculty
desegregation; that they feared Black-White relationships,
especially between Black teachers and White parents and
Black teachers and White students; that they believed
White educators were more favorable toward faculty desegregation than in the past; and that they felt previous
experience in biracial activities would help them adjust
to desegregation.

207. Treiman, D. J. "Status discrepancy and prejudice."
American Journal of Sociology, 71(6), 1966, 651-664.

Treiman examined the effect of status discrepancy on
attitudes toward Blacks by positing an additive model
of the relation between status variables and prejudice
through a dummy-variable multiple-regression procedure
and investigating departures from the predictions of the
model. For two problems, one involving income and education as status variables and the other involving education and education of spouse, using data from a representative national sample of White adults in the United
States, the predictions of the additive model matched
the observed patterns more than the predictions of the
status discrepancy model. (Summary of journal abstract.)

208. Westie, F. R. and Howard, D. H. "Social status differentials and the race attitudes of Negroes." American Sociological Review, 19, 1954, 584-591.

The study was concerned with the attitudes of Blacks
toward Whites and Blacks toward Blacks. The attitude
measure was four social distance scales measuring residential distance, interpersonal distance, position
(positions of power) distance, and physical distance.
The Black sample was made up of males 21 years and over
who were heads of households and who lived in blocks
without Whites. The subjects came from the upper- and
lower-socioeconomic status in order to focus upon the
relationship between social status differences and

attitudes. Interviews were conducted in the homes of
the respondents by a Black interviewer. Results showed
that the higher the status of the subject the less distance he expressed toward Whites in general. Least distance was expressed toward Whites of high status and
greatest toward those of low status. Upper-status Blacks
varied more than lower-status subjects in responses
toward Whites. The responses of the subjects toward
Whites varied according to the area of interaction in
which responses were elicited. Lastly, when the subjects' responses were analyzed in terms of occupational
status, similar results were obtained. For example,
professional and white-collar subjects expressed the
least distance toward Whites in general, while unskilled
workers tended to express the greatest distance.

5

RACIAL ATTITUDES
IN ADULTS

209. Aber, E. M. "A reverse pattern of integration." Journal of Educational Sociology, 32, 1959, 283-289.

Aber was concerned with the effects on the attitudes of
White students of being a minority at a University in
Missouri. A questionnaire was sent to a sample of White
students at the University. All subjects had been in
attendance for at least two semesters. This included
regular, part-time, and graduate students. Some of the
results showed that the respondents generally felt their
experience had given them an improved conception of
Blacks. No student reported that the experience had
increased his prejudice. And only one student reported
having difficulty in adjusting to the situation. This
person felt the attitudes of his friends and relatives
toward his attendance at the university had complicated
his adjustment.

210. Allen, B. P. "Implications of social reaction research
for racism." Psychological Reports, 29(3, Pt. 1), 1971(Dec),
883-891.

Allen asserted that evidence for the existence of racism
would be forthcoming if anti-Black sentiment was shown
to be manifested in social reality in some consistent
way. The Rokeach-Triandis controversy over the primacy
of race or beliefs in prejudice was reviewed in order to
show that past research had yielded a suggestion of a
possible manifestation of racism. An experimental
approach at direct confirmation of this manifestation
was defined. The relationship of the approach to other
actual and possible approaches was described. Finally,
possible misinterpretations of the approach to the study
of racism was delineated. (Summary of article summary.)

211. Allen, V. S. "An analysis of textbooks relative to the
treatment of black Americans." Journal of Negro Education,
40, 1971, 140-145.

The Tau Omega Chapter of the Omega Psi Phi Fraternity
Incorporation chose as a project for the school year
1968-1969 the examination of some of the state approved

course and supplementary textbooks with the objective
of deriving some measurements of how Blacks were treated
in the subject matter. Such things as the number of
pictures of Blacks, their roles, their treatment in
the narrative, and the encouragement of the ideals of
democracy were investigated. Findings were that most
of the characters appearing in the books were White and
of middle-class orientation. Concerning roles, the
Blacks shown were portrayed in low-status positions.
In regard to the investigation of their treatment in
the narrative, it was found that pictures of Blacks
were shown with no reference to the fact in the narrative, persons were shown who had White physical features, only Blacks were shown performing unskilled
labor, they were seldom referred to in the context of
the white-collar work-a-day world, and they were absent
from the various levels of government presented.

212. Allport, G. W. The Nature of Prejudice. Garden City,
New York: Doubleday and Company, Inc., 1958, 496p.

As Allport noted, the book was designed to present a
clarification of the nature of human prejudice including information and examples about its roots, its structure and functioning, and suggested ways to eleviate the
accompanying tensions. The book is divided into the
following sections: Preferential Thinking, Group Differences, Perceiving and Thinking about Group Differences,
Sociocultural Factors, Acquiring Prejudice, The Dynamics
of Prejudice, Character Structure, and Reducing Group
Tensions.

213. Ash, P. "The development of a scale to measure anti-
Negro prejudice." Journal of Social Psychology, 39, 1954,
187-199.

Ash discussed the method used and some of the results
found in the development of a scale to be used to
identify the changes that took place after subjects
watched a film about a variety of issues (social, economic, and health) concerning Blacks and to reflect
responses toward the issues. College students were
asked to write true, false, and own attitude sentences
concerning Blacks in relation to certain topics (voting,
jobs, health, etc.). Sentences which seemed to be distributed from anti-Black through neutral to pro-Black
were selected to be used in each of 13 areas. The sample statements were conspicuous for their almost total
lack of extremeness as found in the Likert (1932) or
Levinson (1950) scales. Furthermore, the experimenter
found a tendency for the statements to be slightly pro-
Black.

214. Athey, K. R., Coleman, J. E., Reitman, A. P., and
Tang, J. "Two experiments showing the effect of the interviewer's social background in responses to questionnaires

concerning racial issues." Journal of Applied Psychology, 44(4), 1960, 244-246.

The authors conducted two experiments in order to determine whether interviewers with different ethnic backgrounds would elicit significantly different responses to questionnaires concerning racial issues. In the first experiment, a White and an Oriental interviewer were used. In the second experiment, a Black and a White interviewer were used. The general results were that there were significantly different responses to the Black and Oriental interviewers by the college sample.

215. Ausubel, D. P. "Ego development among segregated Negro children." Mental Hygiene, New York, 42, 1958, 362-369.

Ausubel found that although the members of the Harlem Black community were fully aware of the unfavorable effects of their segregated environment upon their children, these negative influences were in part compensated by ego-supporting attitudes in the home. (Summary of journal abstract.)

216. Banks, W. M. "The changing attitudes of black students." Personnel and Guidance Journal, 48, 1970, 739-745.

The experimenter studied the racial attitudes of Black college students from a predominately Black university in a border state in order to determine changes in the acceptance or rejection of negative racial stereotypes. The results showed that as a group the subjects accepted more anti-White ideology and less anti-Black ideology than a comparable group of students tested in 1957. The later students were also less authoritarian than the earlier ones. Sex differences showed that males in the present study accepted a greater amount of anti-White ideology than did females.

217. Barron, M. L. American Minorities: A Textbook of Readings in Intergroup Relations. New York: Knopf, 1957, 518p.

The book includes the following subjects: racial psychology, prejudice, racial differences, discrimination in college admissions, authoritarian personality, immigration, integration, organized religion, Protestant-Catholic tensions, religion and class structure, assimilation of ethnic groups, role of police, acculturation in schools, fair employment, definition of nationality, group tensions, and majority and minority Americans in magazine fiction. These topics concern Blacks, Indians, Japanese, Puerto Ricans, Polish, Irish, Italians, and Jewish. (Summary of journal abstract.)

218. Bell, W. and Willis, E. M. "The segregation of Negroes in American cities: A comparative analysis." Social and Economic Studies, 6, 1957, 59-75.

The purpose of the study was to compare the residential
segregation of Blacks in American cities. The data were
obtained from the census trait statistics for the 66
metropolitan areas studied. It was found that the cities
of the South and North Central states were the most
segregated. Other variables related to segregation were
the proportion of the total population represented by
Blacks and the size of the Black population.

219. Berg, K. R. "Ethnic attitudes and agreement of White
persons with a Negro person in the autokinetic situation."
Dissertation Abstracts, 23(1), 1962, 334.

Berg explored the relationship between the attitudes of
Whites toward Blacks and the amount of agreement of a
White person with a Black person in an autokinetic situation. The experimenter hypothesized that the amount of
agreement with a Black person would be directly related
to the amount of attraction toward Blacks and that low
attraction toward Blacks would result in less agreement
in a condition of high salience than in a condition of
low salience. Responses to measures of attraction
toward Blacks were obtained from White, male, college
students. Individual subjects were required to give
autokinetic judgments in a group situation with a Black
and a White confederate. Half of the subjects were told
that a financial reward would be given for accurate
judgments; the other half were not. None of the measures of attraction toward Blacks had the predicted
relationship to agreement with the Black confederate.
And, there was no evidence for the predicted difference
in the amount of agreement under High and Low Salience
conditions.

220. Berreman, G. D. "Race, caste, and other invidious distinctions in social stratification." Race, 13(4), 1972(Apr),
385-414.

Berreman concluded that the concept race as used in the
United States, Europe, and South Africa is not qualita-
tively different in its implications for human social
life than the concepts caste, invisible race, or ethnic
stratification. All of them are distinctions imposed
unalterably at birth upon categories of individuals in
order to justify social distribution of livelihood,
security, power, privilege, freedom, and esteem. The
discontent produced by this deprivation cannot be contained by introducing token flexibility or preaching
brotherly love. Hope only lies in restructuring society and redistributing its rewards in an effort to end
inequality.

221. Bettelheim, B. and Janowitz, M. Social Change and
Prejudice. New York: Free Press Glencoe, 1964, 337p.

Bettelheim and Janowitz discuss the trends in prejudice,
the consequences of social mobility, the psychology of

prejudice, and the theory and practice of social and
personal controls. (Summary of journal abstract.)

222. Bickman, L. and Kamzan, M. "The effect of race and
need on helping behavior." Journal of Social Psychology,
89, 1973, 73-77.

The study examined the effect of race in a situation
where the person in need appealed directly for help.
White female shoppers at supermarkets in New York were
subjects. Women were chosen who were judged to be over
19 years of age and who were unaccompanied. Ten paid
female college students (five White and five Black) were
experimenters. Two experimenters, one of each race, were
present in each of the five supermarkets studied. One
was an observer and the other approached the subject.
The experimenter approached the subject with change in
one hand and the food item (milk for the high need situation and frozen cookie dough for the low need situation)
stating that she did not have the additional 10 cents
needed to buy the item and asking for that amount.
Results were that only need significantly affected helping behavior. Fifty-eight percent of the subjects
helped in the high need condition, and 36 percent in
the low need condition. The White experimenter was
helped 52 percent of the time as compared to 42 percent
for the Black experimenter, but this difference was not
significant.

223. Bird, C., Monachesi, E. D., and Burdick, H. "Infiltra-
tion and the attitudes of white and Negro parents and children." Journal of Abnormal and Social Psychology, 47, 1952,
688-699.

The study was done to measure the reduction of group
tension between Black and White communities in Minneapolis. Black and White parents and children were interviewed by own-race interviewers. Results showed that
dislike of the neighborhood where they lived (because
of the influx of Blacks) generally indicated more prejudice toward Blacks by White families. White males and
females did not differ significantly in their attitudes
toward Blacks and showed more antipathy than regard for
Blacks. According to the analysis of attitudes toward
Jews, both male and female White subjects were more
favorable toward them than toward Blacks. Black respondents were found to have more favorable attitudes toward
Whites, but it was suggested that tolerance built up
over countless lectures and admonitions may have produced these responses. Results for the children showed
that unlike adults, the White youngsters did not manifest more preference for Jews than Blacks, and the mean
scores for attitudes were almost identical toward these
two groups. Black children had more favorable attitudes
toward White children than was the reverse. Black children showed very little prejudice toward non-Jewish White

children but considerable prejudice toward Jewish children. Lastly, parent-child resemblances in racial attitudes were not as close as other relationships involving
attitudes toward institutions.

224. Blake, W. D. "A study of the existence of certain prejudices in the middle years of the adult." Canadian Journal
of Psychology, 6, 1952, 92-94.

Among those prejudices investigated in adult males and
females between the ages of 35 and 65 was that of anti-
Black prejudice. Data were obtained by college students
in a seminar group on psychology of maturity and later
maturity. Results specific to the inquiries about
Blacks were that there was little difference between
the sexes with regard to anti-Black feelings. Additionally, younger subjects were more prejudiced than
older subjects.

225. Blalock, H. M., Jr. "Percent non-white and discrimination in the south." American Sociological Review, 22, 1957,
677-682.

Blalock investigated the relationships between various
indices of discrimination and rate of non-White increase
and percent of non-White in a random sample of 150 southern cities. Indices of discrimination were computed
from 1950 census data. Moderate positive correlations
were found between rate of non-White increase and income
and educational differentials; however, correlations
with other indices of discrimination were not significant. Blalock concluded that the relationship between
discrimination and rate of minority increase was relatively weak.

226. Block, H. D. "Recognition of Negro discrimination: A
solution." Journal of Social Psychology, 48, 1958(Nov),
291-295.

Block discussed the concept of recognition in relation
to racial prejudice and discrimination in terms of an
acknowledgment of the deviation between American social
values and practices. He concluded that recognition may
be either positive or negative with positions between
these two extremes. The position taken along this dimension is determined by social mores. In order to obtain
a rational conformity between values and practice, society must recognize the need for the interdependency of
the social sciences which may help to reveal the depth,
height, and width of the problem.

227. Blodgett, E. G. and Cooper, E. B. "Attitudes of elementary teachers toward Black dialect." Journal of Communication Disorders, 6(2), 1973(Jun), 121-133.

The experimenters administered a questionnaire on attitudes toward Black dialect to White and Black elementary

school teachers in Alabama. The findings were that 50
percent of the Black teachers characterized the dialect
as a complete, but non-standard language. Eighteen percent of the White teachers and 44 percent of the Black
teachers said they were successful in modifying the
dialect. Over 50 percent of the Black teachers and 60
percent of the White teachers suggested that remedial
programs be provided for children with such a dialect.
And 65 percent of the White teachers said they had
trouble understanding the dialect, while 83 percent of
the Black teachers said they had no trouble. Additionally, it was felt that dialect-speaking children were
less intelligent by 50 percent of the White teachers
and 25 percent of the Black teachers.

228. Blood, R. O., Jr. "Discrimination without prejudice."
Social Problems, 3, 1955, 114-117.

The purpose of the study was to examine the relationship
between discriminatory behavior ("overt behavior which
deprives groups of equal access to social facilities
. . .") and prejudiced attitudes ("an attitude involving
an adverse judgment of the abilities, personalities, and
other characteristics of the members of a group") among
White retail employers toward Black employees. It was
suggested that discrimination may be practiced in the
absence of prejudice. The experimenter conducted interviews with the employers on a free-lance basis without
the sponsorship of any agency which might have inhibited
them from expressing their personal opinions. He found
that at neither the sales nor clerical level was there
much evidence that discriminating employers were motivated by beliefs that Blacks were incapable of learning
or performing the necessary skills. The experimenter
noted that the employers had said that while they themselves did not hold prejudiced views some of their
employees did, and to hire Blacks might cause negative
reactions or strikes. It was concluded that real prejudice may not have been tapped or that the motivation for
discrimination might be diverse.

229. Blume, F. R. "The effect of Negro pictorial material
on racial attitudes." Dissertation Abstracts, 28(2-A),
1967, 776.

Blume investigated the effect of viewing photos of
Blacks in traditional stereotyped and/or negative roles
and in positive non-stereotyped roles on subjects' judgments of an individual Black person. Attitudes toward
Blacks were collected from White college students. A
week later subjects were asked to rate from pictures the
character traits of several persons including a Black
individual. Three weeks later subjects were divided
into three groups. One was asked to make up titles to
13 photos, all showing Blacks in negative and stereotyped roles. One was to make up titles for photos of

Blacks in positive roles. And the control group gave
titles to 13 non-Black pictures. Immediately following
this task, subjects rated photos of individuals including the previously rated Black person. It was hypothesized that seeing the pictures would cause a shift in
ratings in the direction suggested in the picture (positive or negative). Also, when level of prejudice was
considered, it was predicted that a differential shift
in ratings would occur with the experimental and control
groups with subjects classified as neutral showing the
largest shift in the direction suggested by the picture.
Differential effects for sex were found for the first
hypothesis with female negative group subjects shifting
significantly in the direction suggested by the picture.
Male subjects were found to be more prejudiced than
females, but the treatment effects were not significant.
A "boomerang" effect was suggested for positive group
females who did not shift significantly in a positive
direction.

230. Boone, J. S.   "The effects of race, arrogance, and evidence on simulated jury decisions." Dissertation Abstracts
International, 33(12-A), 1973(Jun), 7018.

College students were required to read a description of
an assault and robbery of a store owner. They were to
give a verdict with regard to the defendant's guilt, to
sentence the defendant if found guilty, and to state how
they felt personally about the defendant in one of eight
conditions. The conditions were the defendant's race
(Black or White), his courtroom behavior (humble or
arrogant), and the strength of evidence (strong or weak).
The findings were that there were no significant differences in terms of race for judgments of guilt and severity of sentence, but significant race differences for
personal evaluations with Blacks receiving more positive
feelings. There were also significant effects for severity of sentence and evaluations when the defendant was
described as arrogant. Lastly, there were significant
main effects for judgments of guilt and severity of sentence for the evidence condition.

231. Bowman, L. "Racial discrimination and Negro leadership
problems: The case of 'northern community.'" Social Forces,
44(2), 1965, 173-186.

The article was a report of research done in a New
England city where Blacks were in the minority. Problems of discrimination in housing, employment, and school
facilities were found to exist in that city, although
these were not as evident as in many southern communities
or some other northern areas. Bowman asserted that problems of Black leadership appeared to compound the problems of discrimination, or to at least make the search
for solutions more difficult. (Summary of article
abstract.)

232. Brannon, R., et al. "Attitude and action: A field experiment joined to a general population survey." American Sociological Review, 38(5), 1973(Oct), 625-636.

Brannon et al. investigated the relationship between survey-elicited attitudes toward open housing and the willingness to sign and have published a petition consistent with these attitudes among White residents in a metropolitan area in Detroit. The experimenters found that there was a high relationship between attitudes and actions. Three reasons for the greater consistency between attitude and action were hypothesized.

233. Brigham, J. C. "Ethnic stereotypes and attitudes: A different mode of analysis." Journal of Personality, 41(2), 1973(Jun), 206-223.

Brigham suggested that the concept of ethnic stereotype could best be defined as a generalization made about an ethnic group concerning a trait attribution which was considered to be unjustified by an observer. Trait attributes were gathered in regard to Blacks, Whites, and Germans from Black and White college students and from a rural non-college sample of Whites. In addition to making the attributions, the subjects were asked to indicate the range of attributions within which they would consider someone else's trait attribution to be reasonable or justified. They filled out an attitude scale about Blacks. And Black subjects filled out the scale as they thought the typical White college student would. The results indicated that Blacks' perceptions of the typical White student were closer to the expressed attitudes of the rural subjects than to those of the White college subjects.

234. Brigham, J. C. "Racial stereotypes, attitudes, and evaluations of and behavioral intentions towards Negroes and whites." Sociometry, 34(3), 1971(Sep), 360-380.

White male and female subjects were asked to play the part of a juvenile court judge in making evaluations of and assigning sentences to White and Black juvenile offenders. The subjects also completed measures of racial attitudes and stereotyping. Results showed a moderate relationship between the attitude and stereotype measures. These measures were also related to the evaluation of specific Black offenders in terms of their correctable potential and also in terms of the estimated distribution of personality traits. The evaluations were, in turn, related to sentences assigned. But, the attitude measure was only slightly related to treatment, and the stereotype measure was not related to that at all. Thus, the findings were suggested to support the contention of Warner and DeFleur (1969) and others which noted that the relationship between attitudes and behavior was one of

contingent consistency--people behave consonant with
their attitudes only in certain types of situations.

235. Brigham, J. C.   "Racial stereotypes: Measurement variables and the stereotype-attitude relationship." Journal of
Applied Social Psychology, 2(1), 1972(Jan), 63-76.

Brigham found that the ambiguity often associated with
instructions to subjects under the traditional Katz-
Braly paradigm used to assess racial stereotypes did
not act as a major factor in determining responses. The
traits given to five ethnic groups were almost identical
to those given under the instructions used in other studies. Some findings were that, when the White college
students were asked to list the trait-attributes most
commonly used by other people in this society for each
of the ethnic groups presented, the responses concerning
Blacks were different from the subjects' own responses
to Blacks. This discrepancy was not noted for the other
ethnic groups. And, the degree to which a subject's
attributions to Blacks agreed with those seen as most
often used by others in relation to Blacks was positively related to racial prejudice.

236. Brigham, J. C. and Severy, L. J.   "An empirically
derived grouping of whites on the basis of expressed attitudes toward blacks." Representative Research in Social
Psychology, 4(2), 1973(Jun), 48, 55.

The Multifactor Racial Attitude Inventory and the
Marlow-Crowne Social Desirability Scale were given to
undergraduates. People, rather than items, were factor
analyzed according to their responses on the Attitude
Inventory. Each student was assigned to one of four
resulting groups. The students in group one held less
negative racial attitudes. The other students differed
from each other in areas in which the most expressed
racial hostility was evident. Therefore, the students
in group two were most concerned with the social or economic situation facing Blacks. Those in group three
were concerned about aspects of personal interracial
contact. And, students in group four were concerned
with hierarchical status relationships between races.
(Summary of journal abstract.)

237. Brown, W. and Alers, J. O.   "Attitudes of whites and
non-whites toward each other." Sociology and Social
Research, 40, 1956, 312-319.

Brown and Alers conducted a sample survey of the attitudes of White residents of lower Westchester County,
New York, toward non-Whites. It was found that the attitudes were generally favorable, and there was only a
small percentage of harsh racism. For example, a majority of the respondents felt that the Supreme Court's
decision abolishing segregation in public schools would

improve conditions for non-Whites. The small number of
respondents expressing hostile attitudes wished non-
Whites to have equal but separate schools.

238. Buck, J. F. The effects of Negro and white dialectal
variations upon attitudes of college students." Speech
Monographs, 35(2), 1968, 181-186.

The same passage recorded by each of four different
speakers--standard New York dialects as spoken by Black
and White speakers, non-standard dialect as spoken by a
Black speaker, and "New Yorkese" as spoken by a White
speaker--was presented to female college students. The
results suggested that dialectal phonetic variations
affected the listeners' reactions to speech patterns
and to their judgments of a speaker's competence.
(Summary of journal abstract.)

239. Burroughs, W. A. "A study of white females' voting
behavior toward two black female corroborators in a modified
leaderless group discussion." Dissertation Abstracts International, 30(11-A), 1970(May), 5063.

White female college students and two Black female corroborators participated in groups of three (two White
and one of the Black corroborators) in an experiment on
concept problems with a leaderless discussion following
each problem. Burroughs was interested in the number of
votes cast by the White subjects for the Black corroborator as having the most insight into each problem or
as being most likely to have the correct answer. Some
of the results were that the corroborators received more
votes in conditions of high quality performance; the
subjects voted less for the dark-skinned corroborator
who was also more assertive and outgoing (according to
the experimenter's evaluation).

240. Burroughs, W. A. and Jaffee, C. L. "Attitudinal reaction of white females toward two black female collaborators."
Journal of Psychology, 79(1), 1971(Sep), 3-11.

Using a modification of the methodology employed by
Whitacre and Jaffee (1970), Burroughs and Jaffee studied
White female undergraduates' voting behavior in regard
to two Black female confederates. Subjects participated in groups of three including a confederate in a
room separated from an observation room by a one-way
mirror. Conditions of high and low quality of performance by the female confederates were accomplished by
having them follow a script. The conditions of non-
reward, reward, or power were used for the subjects.
The experimental session consisted of 16 problems. For
all groups, the first eight problems were presented
under non-reward conditions, then, depending on the
experimental condition, nine to 16 were presented unre-
warded, rewarded, or with some reception of power.

241. Byrne, D. and Ervin, C. R. "Attraction toward a Negro stranger as a function of prejudice, attitude similarity, and the stranger's evaluation of the subject." Human Relations, 22(5), 1969, 397-404.

Byrne and Ervin conducted an experiment to determine whether attraction to a Black stranger varied directly with the positiveness of the stranger's evaluation of the subject, directly with the proportion of similar attitudes expressed by the stranger, and inversely with the subject's level of racial prejudice. These predictions were confirmed. An unexpected finding was the tendency for highly prejudiced subjects to be more negative to a Black stranger than low prejudiced subjects only under neutral and negative conditions; positive evaluations from the Black stranger mitigated anti-Black prejudice. (Summary of journal abstract.)

242. Caffrey, B. and Capel, W. C. "The predictive value of neutral positions in opinion and attitude research." Journal of Psychology, 69(2), 1968, 145-154.

Female college students were given a scale to measure their attitudes toward Blacks and war in 1935 and in 1965. It was found that students who had neutral attitudes in 1935 maintained that attitude position in 1965. The experimenters suggested that the tendency for investigators to ignore the neutral position on attitude scales or to assign such scores to one of the polar positions was unjustified.

243. Calnek, M. "Racial factors in the countertransference: The black therapist and the black client." American Journal of Orthopsychiatry, 40(1), 1970(Jan), 39-46.

Calnek asserted that racial factors must be acknowledged and dealt with by the therapist. The therapist should not ignore the generalizable cultural attributes of minority members in an effort to emphasize the uniqueness of the individual patient. Few Black Americans have been spared the hurt, grief, sorrow, and anger which has been part of the Black experience; consequently, Calnek feels those who deny these feelings are kidding themselves. Furthermore, since these feelings are the experience of Blacks, they affect the work a Black therapist performs with a Black patient. The Black therapist must examine his own feelings about being Black and his ways of coping with his anger.

244. Campbell, A. White Attitudes Toward Black People. Ann Arbor, Michigan: Institute for Social Research, University of Michigan, 1971, viii, 177p.

Campbell presented a survey of 16- to 69-year-old White residents of 15 cities regarding their attitudes toward Blacks and social action. He reported data on the

interaction of various demographic variables such as
sex, age, and religion on attitudes. (Summary of journal abstract.)

245. Campbell, E. Q. "Moral discomfort and racial segregation: An examination of the Myrdal hypothesis." Social
Forces, 39(3), 1961, 228-234.

Campbell tested the assumption that quiet is associated
with segregation as has been asserted by writers such as
Gunnar Myrdal and Arnold Rose. Southern college students were given a questionnaire on which they were
shown situations involving Blacks. They were to give
responses concerning how they would and ought to behave.
Generally, the results showed that while guilt existed
there were also rationales inherent in the segregated
system which helped to justify segregation behavior.

246. Campbell, E. Q. and Pettigrew, T. F. "Racial and moral
crisis: The role of Little Rock ministers." The American
Journal of Sociology, 64(5), 1959, 509-516.

The authors analyzed the behavior of some Little Rock,
Arkansas, ministers during the problem concerning the
admission of Blacks to Central High School in 1957.
They questioned how these ministers would respond during a racial crisis since they were caught between integrationist ideals and segregationist forces. It was
generally found that the ministers were less vocal and
active in the crisis than one would believe from the
policies of their national church bodies and their own
value systems. However, the authors were surprised to
find that a few of them were vigorous in the face of
congregational disclaim, threats of reprisal, and very
limited support from superiors and peers.

247. Carlson, E. R. "Attitude change through modification
of attitude structure." Dissertation Abstracts, 14, 1954,
726-727.

The experiment tested the prediction that White undergraduates' attitudes toward Blacks or integration of a
White neighborhood would be changed through altering
their perceptions of the importance of the individual
as a means of gaining some value goal. The experimental
procedure required the subjects to take a written test
of objectivity regarding allowing Blacks to move into
White neighborhoods and being part of a discussion on
integration. The results showed that the experimental
manipulation was effective in changing perceptions of
the role of Black housing segregation in attaining the
goals and it changed attitudes toward Black housing for
subjects with moderate pre-experimental attitudes.

248. Carter, R. E., Jr. "Racial identification effects upon
the news story writer." Journalism Quarterly, 36, 1959,
284-290.

Carter was concerned with the effects of knowledge of
the race of a crime suspect on the way a story was written for the newspaper. Matched groups of news-writing
students at three southern and two non-southern universities were required to write crime stories in which the
suspect was or was not identified as a Black person. It
was found that for all subjects, when the suspect was
identified as being Black, the version of the story was
more lenient in terms of evaluation of the guilt of the
individual.

249. Cauthen, N. R.   Robinson, F. E., and Krauss, H. H.
"Stereotypes as contexts of meaning." Proceedings of the
Annual Convention of the American Psychological Association,
6(Pt. 1), 1971, 353-354.

The study investigated the prediction that the words
making up the stereotype of Blacks would shift their
affective meaning when placed in the context of the
stereotype group. In order to assess the possibility
that simply placing a set of words in a human context
would result in a meaning shift, the words were also
presented in the context of a group for whom the words
were unappropriate--Americans. College students were
subjects. In general, a picture was gotten of the Black
stereotype as being neither good nor bad, more potent,
and, in some respects, less active then when presented
within the context of American or simply rated without
reference to a specific type of group.

250. Chestang, L. "The dilemma of biracial adoption."
Social Work, 17(3), 1972(May), 100-105.

Social work's solution to the problem of the thousands
of homeless Black children in the United States has been
biracial adoption. Chestang pointed out that there are
dangers inherent in this approach, both to the Black
child and the White adoptive parent. He did not suggest
that biracial adoptions be abandoned, but he concluded
that in this society only Black families can assure an
environment in which there is an optimal opportunity for
growth, development, and racial identification. (Summary of article abstract.)

251. Clark, E. R. "Patterns of racial stereotypes." Journal of Human Relations, 4(3), 1956, 69-77.

Clark briefly discussed the historical role of various
media (the minstrel show, movies, theatre, music, and
literature) in the perpetuation of Black negative stereotypes. He noted that there would be little objection
to an objective portrayal of group characteristics and
that it was unfortunate that one seldom saw both sides
of Black society.

252. Clark, K. B. "Desegregation: Its implications for
orthopsychiatry." American Journal of Orthopsychiatry, 26,
1956, 445-470.

The article contains discussions by various writers on
such topics as community factors related to desegregation, the role of the community organizer in desegregation, social class factors in public school education as
related to desegregation, the implications for research,
some psychodynamic aspects, and application of a desegregation principle to the treatment of children. (Summary of journal abstract.)

253. Clawson, E. C. "A study of attitudes of prejudice
against Negroes in an all white community." Dissertation
Abstracts, 29(10-A), 1969, 3694-3695.

The aim of the study was to investigate the existence
of prejudice against Blacks in an all White community
where racial contact was limited. Third-, sixth-, and
ninth-grade children were shown matched pairs of pic-
tures--one with Blacks in a social or work situation
and one with Whites in a similar situation. Some of the
results were that children who made prejudicial statements because of the race of the person in the picture
were likely to have negative attitudes toward Blacks in
general. Males were more likely to believe stereotypes
about Blacks and females were more likely to react negatively toward pictured situations of Blacks. And, the
older children were more likely to reject sex-related
integration.

254. Cohen, M. "White students' reactions to the test performance of Negroes." Dissertation Abstracts, 27(1-A),
1966, 249.

Cohen tested two alternative hypotheses: (1) that White
subjects responded less positively toward a Black person
who performed well on a test because he had disconfirmed
their expectations about his behavior, or (2) because he
was a threat to their self-esteem. It was predicted
that subjects working with a White confederate would
respond in terms of expectancy, but subjects working
with a Black confederate would respond in terms of
threat to self-esteem. The dependent variable was the
subject's rescoring of the confederate's final test.
Results showed that the Black confederate received
higher scores than the White confederate.

255. Cohen, O. "The application of social research to intergroup relations." Social Problems, 2, 1954, 20-25.

Cohen discussed the plight of the social science practitioner in trying to sort out the results of much of the
research of race relations and in trying to apply them.
However, social science research findings have had a

great effect upon action in the area of inter-group relations. For example, the study of the techniques of group
dynamics and socio-drama has had an effect upon practical
work. The finding that prejudices are established at an
early age has helped in the encouragement of intercul-
tural educational programs in schools. And the awareness of the importance of the reference group in affecting attitudes and actions has helped practitioners in
their work. Cohen concluded that there should be an
improvement in the methods available for making research
results available to the practitioner and that it was
encouraging to note the extent to which social scientists were gaining first-hand experience of action at
the community level.

256. Coleman, A. L. "Social scientist's predictions about
desegregation: 1950-1955." Social Forces, 38, 1960, 258-
262.

Coleman discussed the role of the social scientist in
making predictions about the course of race relations--
specifically desegregation. He tried to determine all
of the specific predictions made by social scientists
about desegregation which were published during 1950
to 1955. Some of these predictions were that desegregation would occur, that the process would be gradual
and uneven, and that violence would not always accompany this process.

257. Comer, J. P. "White racism: Its root, form, and function." American Journal of Psychiatry, 126(6), 1969, 802-
806.

Comer traced the development of White racism in the
United States to the social and religious environment
of sixteenth-century Europe and the later Revolutionary
era in America. He concluded that without a significant reduction in White racism, Black reaction can only
become more intense and form a basis for widespread and
malignant Black racism.

258. Commission on Race and Housing. Report of the Commission on Race and Housing. Where Shall We Live? Berkeley, California: University of California Press, 1958, 77p.

This report includes the conclusions developed from a
three-year study of racial discrimination in housing.
The following topics are covered: house building, real
estate, finance, property values, social and economic
consequences, law and government, the changing status
of minorities, implications for the future, and the
recommendations of the commission. (Summary of journal
abstract.)

259. Conant, R. W., Levy, S., and Lewis, R. "Mass polarization: Negro and white attitudes on the pace of integration."
American Behavioral Scientist, 2, 1970, 247-263.

The paper focused on a comparison of White and Black attitudes on the pace of change toward integration. A further objective was to find out how education, age, intimate contact with members of the other race, and economic level affected attitudes on the pace of change. Questionnaires were administered in order to determine the attitudes. The findings were that most of the White subjects felt that the pace of integration was about right. Exceptions were to be found with poorly educated, older Whites who had no Black friends. These individuals felt that the pace was too fast. Younger and middle-aged college-educated Whites with Black friends felt the pace was too slow. However, none of the White subjects' scores deviated much from the midpoint of the scale, and no Whites came close to sharing the attitudes of the Black subjects that the pace was too slow. For Black subjects, who had intimate contact with Whites combined with low educational levels and high economic status, there was less dissatisfaction with the pace of change. And, those Blacks who were least satisfied were older and middle-aged, college-educated Blacks.

260. Cook, M. H. "Racial prejudice." World Mental Health, 11, 1959, 90-99.

The article is a compilation of "extracts from authoritative articles" presenting, briefly, essential facts concerning the sources and functions of racial prejudice and discrimination. (Summary of journal abstract.)

261. Cooke, W. H. Peoples of the Southwest: Patterns of Freedom and Prejudice. New York: Anti-Defamation League of B'nai B'rith, 1951, 35p.

The patterns of freedom and prejudice in the southwest were surveyed. The cruelty of the Japanese evacuation and bitter anti-Black attitudes of some immigrants have awakened many citizens. Some of the gains in intergroup relations were outlined. (Abstract summary.)

262. Cothran, T. C. "Negro conceptions of white people." American Journal of Sociology, 56, 1951, 458-467.

Cothran studied the universality, uniformity, and direction of Black people's conceptions of White people. He hypothesized that middle-class Blacks would be more favorable in their conceptions than upper- or lower-class Blacks. From over 200 conceptions secured from Blacks in an open-ended interview, 30 of the most frequently used were put into a modified attitude scale. In terms of universality, it was found that the 30 conceptions were familiar to the majority of subjects. In terms of direction and uniformity, it was found that the lower class was more uniformly unfavorable than the upper and middle classes. And, in general, the conceptions were unfavorable.

263. Cottle, T. J. Black Children, White Dreams. Boston,
Massachusetts: Houghton Mifflin, 1974, 187p.

Cottle presented an account and analysis of the daily
lives of Black children in Boston. He discussed the
ways their lives are affected by the rules of a White
society and how this perception affects their social
and psychological behaviors. (Summary of journal
abstract.)

264. Cox, K. K. "Social effects of integrated advertising."
Journal of Advertising Research, 10, 1970, 41-44.

The same five mass magazines in 1967-1968 had 2 percent
of all their ads integratedly illustrated as compared
with one-half of 1 percent in 1949-1950. And, while
Blacks had been predominantly stereotyped as lower-
skilled laborers in 1949-1950, this was rarely the
case in 1967-1968. (Summary of journal abstract.)

265. Cox, O. C. "Jewish self-interest in 'black pluralism.'"
Sociological Quarterly, 15(2), 1974(Apr), 183-198.

Cox discussed the fact that Jewish tribal exclusiveness
among dominant societal groups has always resulted in
various forms of conflict determined by the social situation. The critical force has been the group's resistance to social assimilation. Different social systems
respond differently to this persistance. Capitalist
culture, for one, has resisted it because it is a basi-
cally assimilationist culture. American Blacks, in
opposing racism, have relied to a large extent on the
ideology of assimilation. The two tendencies have come
into collision and are examined in the article. (Summary of journal abstract.)

266. Crawford, T. J. "Sermons on racial tolerance and the
parish neighborhood context." Journal of Applied Social
Psychology, 4(1), 1974(Jan-Mar), 1-23.

Crawford studied the racial attitudes of White Roman
Catholics in a large midwestern city. The parishioners
were interviewed prior to and following two sermons
opposing racial injustice and segregation. The results
were that there was no significant relationship between
presermon and postsermon attitude change toward integration and the prointegration intensity of the sermons.
Crawford did find, however, that the prointegration
intensity of the sermon was related to the socioeconomic
status of the parishioners. This suggested that the
priests' perceptions of their followers' norms may have
influenced the content of the sermons.

267. Daniel, J. L. "The facilitation of white-black communication." Journal of Communication, 20(2), 1970(Jun),
134-141.

The study was concerned with verbal cues emitted by White
speakers which led to ineffective communication between
Blacks and Whites. The study identified many of the
verbal cues used by Blacks to judge the sincerity of
White speakers. The subjects were a sample of Black
residents of Pittsburgh, Pennsylvania, who were asked
to list the cues they felt they used to judge sincerity.
Some of these verbal cues were: "One of my best friends
is a Negro," "I like you people," and "I grew up in a
Negro neighborhood.

268. Davis, M., Seibert, R., and Breed, W. "Interracial
seating patterns on New Orleans public transit." Social
Problems, 13(3), 1966, 298-306.

The study was done in order to assess the degree of
actual integration on New Orleans Public Service, Incorporation buses during April and May of 1964 in terms of
seating patterns. Three graduate students rode buses
on a number of routes during morning and afternoon peak
hours. Some of the results were that none of the buses
achieved integration so that Whites usually sat in the
front and Blacks in the back. When the bus was over-
crowded, integration was forced to some extent, but this
behavior occurred usually with White males and Black
females. Older people of both races violate the traditional seating pattern less than others, while the
reverse was true for the young.

269. Deane, P. C. "The persistence of Uncle Tom: An examination of the image of the Negro in children's fiction
series." Journal of Negro Education, 37(2), 1968, 140-145.

Deane discussed the persistence of the negative stereotype concerning Blacks in some of the books which are
readily available to children at school or in the stores.
He noted that while certain traits such as the dialect
and certain descriptive or unpleasant connotative terms
had been eliminated from such works, the position in
society, general character, or personality had not been
changed since the beginning of the series of a number
of children's books. Deane concluded that these books
may make a fertile breeding ground for prejudice
through the negative stereotypes.

270. De Fleur, M. L. and Westie, F. R. "The interpretation
of interracial situations: An experiment in social perception." Social Forces, 38, 1959(Oct), 17-23.

De Fleur and Westie reported the findings of an experiment which examined the ways prejudiced and unprejudiced
individuals differed in their perceptions of social
situations involving interactions between pairs of
Blacks and Whites of the opposite sex. Each subject
was shown a set of two color slides portraying the
interracial pair. After seeing the slides, the subjects

were asked certain questions about them. Some of the
results were that there was a tendency for prejudiced
subjects to perceive the Black male-White female slide
as portraying a formal interaction. Female subjects,
regardless of prejudice level, tended to see more roman-
tic themes in the slides than males. And, both groups
of-subjects (prejudiced and unprejudiced) tended to see
the male as leading the action in the Black male-White
female slide in spite of the fact that he was Black.

271. Dell Orto, A. E. and Jordan, J. E. "A multivariate
analysis of racial attitudes: Structure, content, and
determinants." Rehabilitation Psychology, 20(3), 1973(Fal),
126-135.

Dell Orto and Jordan investigated the relationships
between attitude behaviors of Black and White rehabilitation counselor trainees and certain predictor variables. They found that Black and White trainees differed greatly on perceived racial differences, that
geographic location and sex predicted positive attitudes
with females and those born in the North generally being
more positive, and that religion and political preferences were not related to positive attitudes.

272. Dennis, W. "Racial change in Negro drawings." Journal
of Psychology, 69(1), 1968, 129-130.

In 1957 drawings were collected for the experimenter by
a Black psychologist who was teaching an introductory
course in psychology. The drawings were done by Black
students. None of the drawings represented a Black person, all represented Whites. The study was repeated in
1967 with Black students, and it was found that 18 percent of the drawings were of Blacks.

273. Derbyshire, R. L. "United States Negro identity conflict." Sociology and Social Research, 51(1), 1966, 63-77.

Black college students were given a semantic differential test to measure meanings associated with various
ethnic concepts. An insignificant rank-order correlation between social distance and semantic distance shown
by the students for their own group as well as for other
minority and majority groups was interpreted as evidence
of identity conflict. (Summary of journal abstract.)

274. Derbyshire, R. L. and Brody, E. "Social distance and
identity conflict in Negro college students." Sociology and
Social Research, 48(3), 1964, 301-314.

The study was concerned with socio-cultural determinants
of human behavior with reference to problems of identity
and social role. Black college students were given a
modified social distance scale. Attitudes toward other
minorities, Blacks, certain national values, and significant others were also tested. The following hypotheses

were presented: (1) there would be an American Black
group identity, (2) there would be a less potent but significant general Black identity, (3) there would be an
ethnocentric attitude manifested in high school distance
scores toward non-minority group Americans, (4) females
who played a powerful authoritative role in the family
would manifest higher degrees of social distance than
males. Results showed that according to the social distance scores, the subjects saw all groups other than
Blacks as different from themselves. They also saw
groups viewed by Whites as "Black" as being different
from themselves. The subjects produced high accommoda-
tive responses for groups considered to be Black than
non-Black. Highly assimilative (low social distance)
attitudes were shown toward those who resembled the subjects in physiognomy and culture (light-skinned Blacks),
religion, and adherence to American cultural norms
(Canadians). Assimilative attitudes were not based on
skin color; that is, the most accepted non-Black groups
were not the darkest, nor were the least accepted the
lightest. Female subjects had a significantly higher
social distance score than males. Males were more willing to marry light-skinned Blacks and mulattoes than
were females. And, males were more assimilative and
less ethnocentric than females.

275. Dertke, M. C., Penner, L. A., and Ulrich, K. "Observer's reporting of shoplifting as a function of thief's race
and sex." Journal of Social Psychology, 94, 1974, 213-
222.

The authors investigated the reporting of a clearly
observed theft as a function of the race and sex of the
thief and the sex of White observers. The observers
were given the opportunity to either spontaneously
report the shoplifting or to confirm the fact that it
had occurred by responding affirmatively to a direct
question. The results showed that Blacks were reported
or confirmed more often than Whites. (Summary of journal abstract.)

276. Deutsch, M. and Steele, K. "Attitude dissonance among
Southville's influentials." Journal of Social Issues, 15
(4), 1959, 44-52.

Deutsch and Steele conducted a longitudinal study of the
process of desegregation of schools in a southern town.
Middle- and upper-class White adult males and females
were subjects. This group was felt to be the most
articulate and active in community affairs--the most
influential group in the town. Interviews were taken
with each subject. In general, the experimenters found
that staunch segregational attitudes were breaking down
and that there was a sense of acceptance of the inevi-
tability of desegregation.

277. Dodd, J. M. and Strang, H. "A comparison of prejudiced
and non-prejudiced freshman elementary education women."
Journal of Educational Research, 54, 1966, 424-426.

Dodd and Strang attempted to determine whether prejudiced
college students indicated they had certain environmental
backgrounds or personality traits which are different
from students who are not prejudiced. The pilot study
supported a proposed linkage between prejudicial attitudes and social adjustment problems. (Summary of journal abstract.)

278. Dohrenwend, B. S., Colombotos, J., and Dohrenwend, B. P.
"Social distance and interviewer effects." Milbank Memorial
Fund Quarterly, 47(1, Pt. 2), 1969(Jan), 213-226.

Hypothesized that White middle-class interviewers with a
negative attitude toward lower-status persons bias the
answers of Black and White lower-class respondents more
than do counterpart interviewers without this negative
attitude. Analysis of interviewer effect was based on
26 interviewers participating in a community health survey of a sample of 1,713 adults in the Washington Heights
area of New York City. Data for the effects were 22
psychophysiologic items used in the Midtown Study (see
Psychological Abstracts, vol. 38:1031). Results confirm
the hypothesis for all repondents except low-income
Blacks. A second hypothesis examines the effect of two
interviewer attitudes: embarrassment and preference for
high-status respondents. Results are related to the concept of social distance. At either extreme of social
distance, the interviewer effect is likely to be high;
conversely, an optimal middle-social distance may mini-
mize interviewer effects. (Summary of journal abstract.)

279. Donnerstein, E. and Donnerstein, M. "Variables in
interracial aggression: Potential in-group censure." Journal of Personality and Social Psychology, 27(1), 1973(Jul),
143-150.

Two experiments using White male subjects were done to
examine the influence of potential in-group censure and
race of target on aggressive and rewarding responses.
Results showed that the subject gave a lower level of
direct aggression (defined as high shock intensities) to
Black targets under the potential censure condition.
Subjects shocking Whites showed no differential responding as a function of this condition. Additionally,
regardless of the target's race, subjects delivered a
higher level of indirect aggression (longer shock dura-
tions) when in the potential censure condition than
under non-censure. In Experiment II, subjects were
allowed to give monetary rewards of varying amounts for
correct responses and a fixed-intensity shock for incorrect responses. It was hypothesized that subjects
paired with Black targets would give greater rewards

under censure conditions than non-censure because of the
fear of violating nondiscriminatory rules. No such difference was hypothesized for White targets. White male
undergraduates were again used as subjects. Results were
in line' with predictions and showed that subjects gave a
higher level of direct reward to Black targets in the
censure condition; and subjects paired with White targets
did not show differential responding. Increased levels
of indirect aggression were delivered to Black targets
under censure. Subjects paired with White targets did
not exhibit this behavior.

280. Donnerstein, E. and Donnerstein, M. "White rewarding
behavior as a function of the potential for black retaliation." Journal of Personality and Social Psychology, 24(3),
1972(Dec), 327-333.

White male college students were given an opportunity to
give a monetary reward and shock duration to a Black or
White target individual in different conditions of potential retaliation. As was predicted, a higher level of
direct reward was given to Black targets under conditions in which there was a possibility for retaliation
than in conditions which minimized this possibility.
And, as predicted, a high level of indirect aggression
(shock) was given to Black targets in retaliation conditions.

281. Dubey, S. N. "Blacks' preference for black profes-
sionals, businessmen, and religious leaders." Public Opinion
Quarterly, 34(1), 1970, 113-116.

Dubey asked people in a Black neighborhood whether they
would prefer to go to an agency where the director was
Black or White, whether they would rather talk with a
Black or White social worker, whether they would prefer
to be cared for by a Black or White nurse, and other
questions concerning racial preferences in terms of
social services. He found that 77 to 84 percent of the
respondents did not care about the race of the professional person serving them. A strong preference for
Black ministers was expressed by 38 percent of the subjects, but only 10 percent expressed a strong preference
for Blacks in the other positions.

282. Dutton, D. G. "Reactions of restaurateurs to Blacks
and whites violating restaurant dress requirements." Canadian Journal of Behavioral Science, 3(3), 1971(Jul), 298-
302.

The study examined the effects of the race of a customer
on restaurant owners' enforcement of clothing regula-
tions. It was found that when a Black couple entered
the restaurant first, they were served 75 percent of the
time as compared to 30 percent for White couples entering first. And, 38 of 40 owners behaved consistently

to a second couple of the other race when they entered
the restaurant a short time after the first couple.

283. Dutton, D. G. and Lake, R. A. "Threat of own prejudice
and reverse discrimination in interracial situations."
Journal of Personality and Social Psychology, 28(1), 1973
(Oct), 94-100.

The study tested the prediction that reverse discrimination (more favorable behavior by Whites toward minority
group individuals than toward other Whites) would result
from the observation by Whites of threatening cues of
prejudice in their own behavior. White males and females
who had rated themselves as unprejudiced were subjects.
Subjects were put in either a high-threat or low-threat
condition and autonomic behavior was measured. After
this, the subjects were panhandled by a Black or a White
confederate. Results showed that the Black panhandler
received more money from subjects in the high-threat
condition, and there was no difference in the contribu-
tions to the White panhandler by subjects in either
condition.

284. Eddy, E. M. "Attitudes toward desegregation among
southern students on a northern campus." Journal of Social
Psychology, 62(2), 1964, 285-301.

The study was concerned with the attitudes toward desegregation of northern and southern freshmen and seniors
on a northern college campus in order to test the prediction that southern seniors were more liberal than
southern freshmen. A 53-item questionnaire was administered to provide information about such things as the
socioeconomic status of the subject's parents, the
region of the country in which the subject had been born
and schooled, and the region of the country in which the
parents had attended college. Attitudes toward Blacks
and desegregation were also obtained by the questionnaire. The results showed that the hypothesis was more
true of students from the Deep South than from border
states. Additionally, Deep South subjects' attitudes
were differentiated according to socioeconomic status
and intent to remain in the North with subjects with
comparatively limited socioeconomic status and those
planning to remain in the North being more liberal.
Lastly, border state subjects' attitudes were related
to participation in extracurricular activities and the
regional origin of college friends; subjects participating in a greater number of activities and subjects
whose best friends were northerners were more liberal.

285. Ehrlich, H. J. "Stereotyping and Negro-Jewish stereotypes." Social Forces, 41(2), 1962, 171-176.

The purpose of the study was to examine the difference
between stereotyping as a process and stereotype

assignment which applies to the selection of a target
and content of the stereotypes. White undergraduates
were subjects who were asked to sort statements about
people in general into one of four categories indicating
the statement was applicable to Blacks, Jews, both, or
neither. The findings were that the content of Jewish
and Black stereotyping was distinctive and mutually
exclusive; however, the number of Black and Jewish stereotypes endorsed were moderately highly correlated.
Thus, generality seemed to be shown in the subjects'
willingness to stereotype and the relationship between
the number endorsed.

286. Ehrlich, H. J.   "The study of prejudice in American
social science." The Journal of Intergroup Relations, 3(2),
1962(Apr), 117-125.

Ehrlich pointed out that in a society in which a high
value is placed on equality, tolerance, and human dig-
nity, any indication of inequality, intolerance, and
inhuman treatment of others is regarded as socially
pathological. The extent of this problem in intergroup relations can be documented quite easily by sur-
veying opinions and pursuing statistics; however,
Ehrlich felt it was more important to attempt to determine the causes and possible preventions of this phenomenon. He discussed such topics as the "Functions of
Stereotypes," the transmission of racial attitudes,
prejudiced persons, "Prejudice and Intergroup Behavior,"
"Some Psychological Mechanisms" of prejudice, and
"Guidelines for Community Programs."

287. Elkind, D.   "From ghetto school to college campus:
Some discontinuities and continuities." Journal of School
Psychology, 9(3), 1971, 241-245.

Elkind discussed some of the continuities and discontinuities faced by Black students coming from a ghetto
school to a predominantly White, middle-class college.
Some of the continuities encountered are a lack of
preparation on the part of White high school and college teachers for dealing with Black students; confusion
on the part of teachers and administrators about education and racial prejudice; and lack of Black male teachers to act as role models. One of the discontinuities
is a school culture dominated by a Black majority and a
culture in the ghetto school versus a college dominated
by the White majority and culture.

288. English, W. H.   "Minority group attitudes of Negroes
and implications for guidance." Journal of Negro Education,
26, 1957, 99-107.

The aim of the study was to determine the extent and
depth of minority group attitudes among Blacks in
Springfield, Massachusetts. A free group discussion

was recorded and analyzed for the expressed attitudes.
English concluded from the results of the study that
there was a subculture among these Black residents which
was so deeply imbedded beneath their conscious level of
expression that it could not be detected in the verbal-
ized content. This conclusion was drawn because of the
noticeable restraint used by the discussants whenever
race was introduced as a topic. English suggested that
this restraint may have been a result of the fact that
these individuals felt their minority status so deeply
that they were unwilling to reveal their feelings, even
to each other.

289. Erskine, H. "The polls: Recent opinion on racial
problems." Public Opinion Quarterly, 32(4), 1968-1969, 696-
703.

The experimenter presented data gathered in May or June,
1968, by the Gallup organization concerning various
aspects of race relations. Some of the questions and
results were as follows: Question--The conclusion of
the President's Commission of Civil Disorders was that
our nation is moving toward two societies, one Black and
one White, separate and unequal. Do you agree with their
conclusion, or not? Responses--The national total who
agreed was 36 percent, those disagreeing 51 percent, and
those with no opinion 13 percent. Responses by Whites
only--Agree, 36 percent; disagree, 52 percent; and no
opinion, 12 percent. By sex for Whites--males agreeing,
31 percent; males disagreeing, 53 percent; and males no
opinion, 15 percent. And, question--In your opinion,
how well do you think Blacks are being treated in this
community--the same as Whites, not very well, or badly?
Responses--The national totals were: same, 70 percent;
not very well, 17 percent; badly, 3 percent; and no
opinion, 10 percent. Responses for Whites--same, 73
percent; not very well, 14 percent; badly, 3 percent;
and no opinion, 10 percent. Responses by sex for
Whites--males, same, 70 percent; males, not very well,
17 percent; males, badly, 4 percent; and males, no
opinion, 9 percent; women, same, 69 percent; women,
not very well, 18 percent; women, badly, 3 percent;
and women, no opinion, 10 percent.

290. Ewens, W. L. "Reference other support, ethnic attitudes, and perceived influence of others in the performance
of overt acts." Dissertation Abstracts International, 30
(2-A), 1969, 806.

The problem concerned the way reference others and
racial attitudes (toward Blacks) influenced behavior.
White undergraduates were subjects. Some of the findings were that the students reported that they did not
consciously consider the expectations of others when
deciding how to behave in the experiment. And, racial
attitudes were found to be related to reference other
support and to overt behavior.

291. Fagan, J. and O'Neill, M. "A comparison of social distance scores among college student samples." Journal of
Social Psychology, 66(2), 1965, 281-290.

The study was done to point up recent trends in social
distance attitudes and to serve as a basis for assessing
changes since 1953. It was hypothesized that there would
be differences in social distance scores among students
at different Georgia colleges and that there would be
differences in scores between Georgia college samples
tested in 1953 and 1962. The following groups of subjects were used: Blacks from a private Black college,
White students from a state college, White nursing students, White males from a predominately male college,
and White females from a predominately female college.
The Bogardus Social Distance Scale was administered during class times. Results showed that within the five
groups of subjects three distinct populations appeared.
The Black subjects differed significantly from the four
White groups; the nursing group differed significantly
from the other groups; and the male, female, and coed
groups did not differ significantly from each other.
An investigation of results for 1953 showed that the
male, female, and coed groups were similar in that they
showed the least social distance toward Protestants,
Democrats, English, Republicans, and Canadians and the
most distance toward Socialists, Blacks, and Communists.
A comparison of ranking for the two years investigated
showed that the 1965 coed male-female group indicated
lower mean ratings than the 1953 subjects. The ratings
given to the 16 groups either decreased or remained the
same except for Blacks, Cubans, and Filipinos. Like-
wise, the average social distance ranking by Black subjects in the present study was lower with only two
groups--Cubans and Blacks--showing an increase in
social distance.

292. Fauman, S. J. "Housing discrimination, changing neighborhoods, and public schools." Journal of Social Issues,
13(4), 1957, 21-30.

Fauman discussed some of the factors involved in housing
discrimination, changing neighborhoods, and the role of
schools in stratifying membership, curriculum, and
extracurricular activities. Statements were presented
which would hopefully be tested. These statements concerned, for instance, that notion that neighborhoods
would continue to strive to achieve homogeneity in
status, that an area marked by one ethnic clustering
would disperse and recluster when penetrated by another
ethnic group, and that ethnic, religious, racial groups
even under conditions of equality of access to housing
by socioeconomic level would continue to cluster in
specific areas at any class level.

293. Fendrich, J. M. "A study of the association among
verbal attitudes, commitment, and overt behavior in

different experimental situations." Social Forces, 45(3),
1967, 347-355.

Fendrich examined the relationship between expressed
racial attitudes and overt behavior looking at characteristics of the research setting which might influence
the expression of attitudes and affect the consistency
between verbal and overt behavior. Overt behavior was
measured by the degree to which college students volun-
tarily became socially involved in a campus chapter of
a civil rights organization. The results were that the
structure of the experimental situation in which verbal
attitudes were measured determined whether there would
be consistency between verbal attitudes and overt
behavior.

294. Fendrich, J. M. "Perceived reference group support:
Racial attitudes and overt behavior." American Sociological Review, 32(6), 1967, 960-970.

The study was done to explore the paired relationships
among perceived reference group support, racial attitudes, and overt behavior. It was also concerned with
exploring how well the data which were obtained would
fit each of four three-variable theoretical models suggested by previous researchers. The subjects used in
the study were college students who were active in the
community. The data were found to fit the fourth model
best which assumes that perceived reference group support determines both racial attitudes and overt behavior but that racial attitudes are a partially independent determinant of overt behavior.

295. Fenelon, J. R. and Megargee, E. I. "Influence of race
on the manifestation of leadership." Journal of Applied
Psychology, 55(4), 1971, 353-358.

The experimenters investigated whether racial differences could influence the manifestation of dominance by
pairing Black and White, high- and low-dominance females
and requiring them to interact in a task in which one
would lead and the other follow. It was found that the
rate of leadership assumption by high-dominance White
females paired with low-dominance Black females was
lower than the rate of assumption by high-dominance
subjects in other groups. This was interpreted in
terms of the White females' reluctance to dominate
a low-dominance Black female and the Black females'
increased assertiveness with a White partner.

296. Fishbein, M. "An investigation of the relationship
between beliefs about an object and the attitude toward
that object." Human Relations, 16(3), 1963, 233-239.

Fishbein tested the prediction that an individual's
attitude toward an object is a function of his beliefs

about the object and the evaluative aspects of those
beliefs. College undergraduates were subjects.
Responses to the word "Negro" were obtained from the
subjects. The 10 most frequent characteristics were
used to construct 10 belief statements. Later, a
smaller group of subjects rated each characteristic,
each belief statement, and the concept "Negro." The
results supported the hypothesis.

297. Fishman, J. A. "Some social and psychological determinants of intergroup relations in changing neighborhoods:
An introduction to the Bridgeview study." Social Forces,
40, 1961, 42-51.

The article reviewed recent social science literature
on intergroup relations in changing neighborhoods and
illustrated this information with reference to a recently
completed study of entry by Blacks into Bridgeview, a
suburb in New Jersey. It was found that the overt
responses of Blacks and Whites toward each other were not
in agreement with their intergroup attitudes. Fishman
wrote that the entry of minority groups into neighborhoods where such groups had not previously resided was
not only disruptive of the status needs and assumptions
of earlier residents, but also of their images of the
neighborhood.

298. Forbes, G. B. and Mitchell, S. "Attribution of blame,
feelings of anger, and direction of aggression in response
to interracial frustration among poverty-level female Negro
adults." Journal of Social Psychology, 83, 1971, 73-78.

Forbes and Mitchell investigated adult Black females'
reactions to interracial frustration. It was predicted
that the subjects would attribute more blame to the
frustrator in a situation in which a White person frustrates a Black than when the race of the frustrator is
reversed, subjects would report more anger when a White
person frustrates a Black person, and they would show
more outward direct aggression when a White person frustrates a Black person. Only the first prediction was
supported.

299. Frazier, E. F. "Areas of research in race relations."
Sociology and Social Research, 42, 1958, 424-429.

Frazier pointed out that the field of race relations has
long been one of the major concerns of American sociolo-
gists. He noted that their interest in this field had
been changing partly because of the developments which
occurred in race relations in the United States and
because of changes in the entire world. In light of
their changing interest and perspective, Frazier suggested some sociological problems which he felt needed
further study: the problem of race sentiment and
consciousness, the role of social sentiment and

consciousness in personality formation, and the influence of institutions on race relations and racial attitudes.

300. Fromkin, H. L., Klemoski, R. J., and Flanagan, M. F.
"Race and competence as determinants of acceptance of new-
comers in success and failure work groups." Organizational
Behavior and Human Performance, 7(1), 1972(Feb), 25-42.

The purpose of the study was to determine the effects of
the race and competence of a newcomer on his acceptance
into a work group. Black and White male undergraduates
were subjects. The groups were composed of three members who worked on a judgmental task and got feedback
on the groups' success or failure. Later, Black or White
newcomers were introduced into the group under high- or
low-task competency. A postexperimental questionnaire
was administered in order to assess the groups' reactions
to the newcomer. It was found that high-competent newcomers were more preferred, regardless of their race or
the groups' performance feedback. Success groups' preferences were generally based on the newcomer's attribution of task competency, while nonsuccess groups' refer-
ences were based on the newcomer's task competency and
race.

301. Gaertner, S. and Bickman, L. "Effects of race on the
elicitation of helping behavior: The wrong number technique." Journal of Personality and Social Psychology, 20(2),
1971, 218-222.

The field study was done to indicate the extent to which
racial attitudes affected helping behavior in adults.
The subjects were residents of Brooklyn, New York, sam-
pled from the telephone directory. Black subjects were
chosen according to last name and area of residence, and
as a final check, voice characteristics. White subjects
were chosen only according to geographic location. To
insure that male and female subjects would be home to
receive the calls, the study was done between the hours
of 6:30 and 9:30 P.M. The caller (a male confederate)
pretended to be trying to contact "Ralph's Garage"
because he was stuck on the parkway and needed a mechanic
to come look at his car. Results showed that White subjects helped the White victim more often than they helped
the Black victim by calling the garage (the number was
actually that of an experimental assistant acting as a
garage attendant). Among Black subjects, White victims
were given more help than Black victims; however, the
difference was not statistically significant. By sex,
it was found that Black females helped White victims more
often than Black victims, while Black males helped Black
and White victims equally as much. Both male and female
White subjects helped White victims more often than Black
victims. White male and female subjects tended to hang
up prematurely more frequently on the Black than White

victims. Sex differences for premature hang ups showed
that females hung up prematurely more often than did males.

302. Gittler, J. B. Understanding Minority Groups. New
York: John Wiley, 1956, 139p.

The book includes eight lectures by various social scientists. Some of the topics covered are the ethical
aspects of group relations, the role of Jews in America,
the movement to enhance the status of Blacks, and the
effects of discrimination on the personality of minorities. The latter topic is discussed by Gittler. (Summary of journal abstract.)

303. Golden, J. "Social control of Negro-white intermar-
riage." Social Forces, 36, 1958, 267-269.

Golden discussed some of the pressures put upon Blacks
and Whites who intermarry. The most obvious pressures
are the laws which prohibit such marriages and the social
structure of the society, but there are also pressures
from clerks issuing licenses, clergymen, army officers,
and the families of the individuals involved. In light
of these restrictions, why do some of these marriages
take place? Golden suggested that there are factors in
our society which operate to lessen the effectiveness of
these social controls. He said that these factors would
be discussed in a later study.

304. Goldstein, M. W. "Race and belief prejudice: A further
interpretation concerning the relationship between norms and
behavioral intentions." Dissertation Abstracts International,
31(1-A), 1970(Jul), 465.

The study by Goldstein was a continuation of one done in
1965 by Triandis and Davis. These two experimenters
differed with Milton Rokeach concerning the importance
of belief or race similarity in regard to reactions
toward a stimulus person. Goldstein predicted that the
findings by Triandis and Davis would be replicated, that
race would account for an increasing percent of the vari-
ance for belief prejudice and race prejudice subjects as
behavioral items on a questionnaire became more intimate,
that there would be a difference between these types of
subjects in regard to the importance of race or belief
similarity of a stimulus person, and that subjects would
perceive important social groups as increasingly prohib-
iting contacts with the stimulus person. Individuals
from Rider Community and Hunter colleges were subjects
and the predictions were confirmed.

305. Goodman, P. "Reflections on racism, spite, guilt, and
violence." In The New York Review of Books, May 23, 1968.
Pp. 18-23.

Goodman discussed some of the aspects of Black and White
prejudice in his article and made the following

observations: The White middle class is not so much
racist (toward Blacks and other minorities which they
considered to be strange) as narrow, self-righteous, and
busy; Blacks are by and large racist; and while Whites
are able to disregard Blacks, Blacks cannot disregard
the power of Whites which controls every aspect of their
lives.

306. Gordon, M. M.   "Recent trends in the study of minority
and race relations."   The Annals of the American Academy of
Political and Social Science, 350, 1963(Nov), 148-156.

The author summarized and commented on some of the trends
in the study of minority groups and race relations within
the United States. His article was primarily focused
upon works published between 1958 and 1963.

307. Grafton, T. H.   "An attitude scale on accepting Negro
students."   Social Forces, 43(1), 1964, 38-41.

A Thurstone-type attitude scale was constructed in order
to measure attitudes among the all White students at a
southern college for women on the hypothetical question
of accepting a Black student. The experimenter found
that there was greater opposition to a Black student
entering the school by southern than by border state or
northern students. Freshmen were more opposed to the
entry than older students.

308. Gray, J. S. and Thompson, H. H.   "The ethnic prejudices
of white and Negro college students."   Journal of Abnormal
and Social Psychology, 48, 1953, 311-313.

The study made a comparison of White undergraduates in a
southern university with Black students in three southern Black colleges using a modified version of the Bogardus social distance scale. The subjects were to rate 24
ethnic groups on an eight-point scale. An anonymous personal data measure was also given. It was found that
Black subjects rated all groups, except their own, lower
than did White subjects. It was also found that acquain-
tance with at least five members of an ethnic group (as
determined from the personal data information) raised
the social distance ratings of Black and White subjects
for that group. The one exception concerned Mexicans.
Other factors such as age, education, and education of
Black parents also affected social distance ratings so
that freshmen were less liberal than seniors, older students were less liberal than younger ones, and Blacks
whose parents were college graduates were more liberal
than those whose parents were high school graduates.
Income of parents and religion did not have an affect
on ratings. The same social distance scale was given
to high school students and adults in order to check
the reliability of the data, and similar results were
obtained.

309. Greeley, A. M. and Sheatsley, P. B. "Attitudes toward racial integration." Scientific American, 225(9), 1971(Dec), 13-19.

The article presented the third report on the findings of the National Opinion Research Center concerning the attitudes of Whites toward the position Blacks should occupy in American society. The Center's sampling covered a 30-year period, and it was found that the trend of White attitudes has been moving strongly toward the approval of integration. And, although a negative reaction to Black militancy was observed, this did not seem to impede the steady increase in the proportion of White Americans willing to endorse integration. Additionally, by region, it was found that southern Whites' attitudes have also become more favorable toward integration, especially on transportation and in schools.

310. Green, M. W. "Interrelationships of attitude and information: A study based on the responses of southern white high school students to questions about the Negro." Dissertation Abstracts, 14, 1954, 1839-1840.

The study investigated some of the interrelationships between attitude and information, the influence of initial attitude on the learning of relevant information, and the effect of having learned new information about attitudes. Scales measuring attitudes and information about Blacks were given to southern White ninth- and tenth-graders. Next, they were required to read paragraphs giving information about Blacks. Then the information and attitude scales were readministered. It was found that there was a relationship between level of knowledge about Blacks and the subjects' attitudes toward them and that although initial attitudes do not exert an outstanding influence upon the learning of new material, there was the suggestion of a relationship, and the possession of new information was associated with increases in favorable attitudes.

311. Gregor, A. "Race relation, frustration, and aggression." Revue Internationale de Sociologie, Série 2, 2(2), 1965, 90-112.

Gregor reviewed research findings pertaining to the sociogenesis of aggressive attitudes and conduct disorders in Blacks. The origin, nature, and extent of prejudice directed toward Blacks are examined and explained in terms of in-group versus out-group identity which is seen as essential to the development of self-esteem which in turn determines the development of aggressive attitudes. Gregor noted that the minority group child who accepts majority values, rejects his own group. This type of attitude is incompatible with a self-system which affords maximum ego strength. He suggested steps which might be taken in order to better race relations.

312. Grodzins, M. "Metropolitan segregation." Scientific American, 197(4), 1957, 33-41.

Grodzins discussed the new pattern of segregation which was developing as Blacks moved in from the South and Whites moved out to the suburbs. These population shifts bring profound economic consequences: a decline in central city business activity and associated property values, and a movement to the suburbs of corporation offices, banks, law firms, and businesses which serve them. A political development in the organization of Blacks for ends conceived narrowly to the advantage of the Black community.

313. Grossack, M. M. "Group belongingness among Negroes." Journal of Social Psychology, 43, 1956, 167-180.

Grossack pointed out that a great deal of theoretical and empirical evidence has suggested that belonging to an underprivileged minority has negative consequences on individual members. He reviewed the literature on this topic and discussed Blacks' characterizations of their group membership. Lastly, he presented a theory of minority group belongingness.

314. Grossack, M. M. "Perceived Negro group belongingness and social rejection." Journal of Psychology, 38, 1954, 127-130.

The study was designed to test the following predictions: (1) Attraction to the group is an ideal social norm shared by Blacks, (2) individuals typifying positive group belongingness will be accepted by Blacks; and (3) individuals deviating from this norm of belongingness will be socially rejected by Blacks. These predictions were tested by using a hypothetical social situation presented in story form. The results showed that the predictions were supported.

315. Group for the Advancement of Psychiatry, Committee on Social Issues (New York City). "Psychiatric aspects of school desegregation." Group for the Advancement of Psychiatry Report, 37, 1957, 95p.

This report consists of three sections--introduction, psychodynamics of responses to desegregation, and a summary and discussion. It treats with the functions of racial myths and prejudices, the psychodynamics of changing attitudes, and the role of authority in the changing of attitudes and behavior. The responses of various groups to desegregation are considered in relation to children, the parents, and the educators. (Summary of journal abstract.)

316. Halper, I. S. "The counterpoint of racial and oedipal themes in the psychotherapy of a Negro patient." Psycho-analytic Review, 57(2), 1970, 169-180.

Halper discussed the counterpoint of racial and oedipal
themes in the psychotherapy of a Black theology student.
In the initial stages of therapy, the man's Uncle Tom
facade and clown-like appearance concealed aggressive
and competitive tendencies. His conflicts seemed to be
related to social conditions in the South during his
childhood as well as to early psychosexual development
and the Oedipus complex. Halper also discussed the difficulties in the treatment of Black patients by White
psychiatrists although the racial difference between the
present patient and therapist was not a major obstacle
in the therapy. (Summary of article summary.)

317. Hamm, N. H., Williams, D. O., and Dalhouse, A. D.
"Preference for black skin among Negro adults." Psychological Reports, 32(3, Pt. 2), 1973(Jun), 1171-1175.

The experimenters conducted a study to test the hypothesis that Blacks place a positive value on dark skin
color. It was additionally hypothesized that younger
subjects would be more positive toward dark skin than
older subjects. Subjects were males in the age groups
15-25, 35-45, and 55-65 from a Black community. Subjects were required to chose a face which they felt was
most like their own and to chose a face they felt was
the nicest or the most beautiful from among 11 cardboard
faces varying in skin color (one white and 10 ranging
from tan to dark brown). All of the faces were homo-
geneous except for color. The experimenter rated each
subject's color using as a standard the 10 cardboard
stimuli. For another task, each subject was required
to choose from among 20 stimulus figures (10 representing Whites and 10 of different skin tones representing
Blacks) those described in five situations devised by
the experimenter. Pre-experimental ratings of the relative darkness of each skin color for the Black stimulus
materials were used in calculating the dependent measures. Some of the results were that: (1) subjects
were realistic in their face choices; (2) no significant
preference on the part of all subjects for darker skin
colors nor an increasing tendency for older subjects to
prefer lighter tones was found; (3) for the choose-a-
person task, more positive behavior characteristics were
attributed to dark skin figures than negative characteristics; and (4) a main effect for age showed that the
young group attributed more positive behavior characteristics to the dark-skinned stimulus than did the intermediate and older groups.

318. Hannerz, U. "The rhetoric of soul: Identification in
Negro society." Race, 9(4), 1968, 453-466.

Hannerz discussed the social and cultural implications
of the emergence of the concept "soul." The historically
impermeable barriers to the advancement of Blacks have
been slightly lowered to make success possible. This

change has created the need for a philosophic alternative to the type of success defined by mainstream, White
ideals; the concept of soul provides an appreciation for
Blackness. It is an internal, cultural concept rather
than a movement such as Black militancy. However, as a
cultural force, it could be harnessed to create alle-
giance to a Black nationalist political movement.
(Summary of journal abstract.)

319. Harding, J. (Ed.)   "Intergroup contact and racial attitudes." Journal of Social Issues, 8(1), 1952, 72p.

Six studies of involuntary contact between adults of
various groups was presented from the program of the
Commission of Community Interrelations of the American
Jewish Congress and the Research Center of Human Relations of New York University. Some of the topics were
Mexicans and Puerto Ricans in a Utah mining town, attitudes toward Black co-workers in an Eastern urban
department store, treatment of Blacks in a West Virginia
mining area, and the effects of Blacks at varying distances from White neighbors in housing projects. (Summary of journal abstract.)

320. Hartsough, W. R. and Fontana, A. F.   "Persistence of
ethnic stereotypes and the relative importance of positive
and negative stereotyping for association preferences."
Psychological Reports, 27(3), 1970(Dec), 723-731.

The experimenters compared data from 1932, 1950, and
1961 in order to examine the stereotyping of 10 ethnic
groups by American college students. Although there
was a good deal of variation among the time periods,
core stereotypes were found for eight groups. For
Blacks, for example, the stereotype of the Black person
as an intellectual inferior was not reported in the sample. The traits ignorant and stupid were not applicable
and supersititious, lazy, and very religious were used
less. Increase in the use of traits such as musical,
showy, happy-go-lucky, and pleasure-loving were suggested to be related to the presentation of Black performers on records and television.

321. Hausrath, A. F.   "Utilization of Negro manpower in the
army." Journal of the Operations Research Society of America, 2, 1954, 17-30.

Hausrath discussed the factors affecting the decision to
integrate Blacks into previously all White army units.
The particular factors were statistics of scores on the
Army General Classification Test, Black and White performance in combat, and the interactions between Black
and White soldiers as determined by opinions, attitudes,
actual behavior, and critical incidents. It was concluded that integrated units could make more effective
use of manpower than segregated units, that resistance

to integration is reduced as experience in integrated
units is gained, and that levels of 20 percent Blacks
were more acceptable. Hausrath also discussed the time
required to extend integration to the whole Army.
(Summary of journal abstract.)

322. Heller, C. and Pinkney, A. "The attitudes of Negroes
toward Jews." Social Forces, 43(3), 1965, 364-369.

The experimenters analyzed data from the Newsweek 1963
Poll of American Blacks' attitudes toward the role of
Jews in the cause of Black rights. Interviews were conducted by Newsweek with Black men and women randomly
selected throughout the United States. Additionally,
100 Black leaders were interviewed. The findings were
that, in general, the attitudes of Blacks on the stand
of Jews was more favorable than unfavorable. However,
49 percent of the respondents indicated that they were
not sure. Blacks outside the South expressed more favorable attitudes toward the role of Jews in the Black
civil rights struggle than did Blacks in the South.
But, this difference in response was accounted for by
the greater reluctance of southern Blacks to express
themselves rather than their greater willingness to say
that Jews were harmful. Analysis of the leader's
responses showed that 71 percent felt that Jews were
more helpful and only 8 percent felt they were more
harmful. In general, those Blacks with the most favorable attitudes were the leaders and had higher
incomes. Those with low incomes and education levels
and those who lived in the rural South had less favorable attitudes.

323. Hendrick, C. and Rumenik, D. K. "Race versus belief
about race as determinants of attraction: Belief prejudice and two kinds of race prejudice." Journal of Experimental Research in Personality, 7(2), 1973(Sep), 148-164.

Hendrick and Rumenik investigated the effects of racial
membership versus similarity of beliefs about racial
issues on interpersonal evaluations. Prejudiced and
unprejudiced White male college students observed a
videotaped interaction of two Black and two White male
actors discussing racial issues. They then rated the
actors on several scales. One actor of each race took
a conservative position on the issues and the other two
took a liberal position. The findings showed that prejudiced subjects were attracted to the conservative
actors, while unprejudiced students were attracted to
the liberal actors. Prejudiced subjects preferred the
White actor; however, unprejudiced subjects preferred
the Black actor.

324. Hicks, J. M. "The validation of attractiveness judgments as an indirect index of social attitude." Journal of
Social Psychology, 88(2), 1972(Dec), 307-308.

The purpose of the study was to validate attractiveness
judgments as an indirect index of attitudes toward Blacks
by using the convergent-discriminant procedure. The procedure involved correlating "Attractiveness Judgments of
Negroes" with "Attitudes Toward Negroes," correlating
"Attractiveness Judgments of Whites" with "Attitudes
Toward Negroes," and making a statistical comparison of
the two kinds of coefficients. Subjects were White male
and female undergraduates from a midwestern state university. Stimulus materials were front-view facial pictures
of Black and White males and females and a Likert measure
of attitudes toward Blacks. The pictures were chosen
from college annuals to represent a range of attractiveness. Subjects rated same and opposite sex pairs. The
names of the subjects were obtained. The results showed
that for White subjects attractive judgments of Black
males may be used as an indirect measure of racial attitudes. There were no significant correlations for Black
females. The experimenter noted that the discrepancy
indicated that perhaps attitudes toward Blacks, as traditionally measured, were more closely associated with
Black males than with Black females.

325. Himelstein, P. and Moore, J. C.   "Racial attitudes and
the action of Negro and White background figures as factors
in petition signing." Journal of Social Psychology, 61(2),
1963, 267-272.

The experimenters explored a particular attribute of a
confederate (race or color) as a factor in influencing
subjects' behavior in a petition signing situation.
They hypothesized that among White southern college
students attitudes toward a Black confederate would be
reflected in their reaction to a petition after the confederate had either signed or refused to sign the petition. Thus, for subjects with high scores on an attitude measure, signing or not signing would tend to be
the reverse of that of the Black confederate.

326. Himes, J. S. Racial and Ethnic Relations. Dubuque,
Iowa: Wm. C. Brown, 1974, 61p.

Himes presented an introduction to the sociology and
psychology of racial and ethnic social structures in
the United States. He emphasized the changing patterns
of relations among minority and majority groups. The
topics covered were the demographic and socioeconomic
characteristics of American minorities, minority sub-
cultures, the social organization of minorities, and
the politics of minority status. (Summary of journal
abstract.)

327. Hines, R. H. "Social distance components in integration attitudes of Negro college students." Journal of Negro
Education, 37(1), 1968, 23-30.

The study tested the social distance attitudes of Black
college students in terms of integration. The subjects
were given one question in which they were to chose
between Blacks and Whites or to indicate indifference to
nine hypothetical situations. A second part of the
questionnaire required that they rank six racial-ethnic
groups in terms of their preference for participation.
Finally, they were to rank Whites, Jews, American
Indians, Mexicans, and Chinese in order of preference.
The results showed that the students preferred Whites
over other racial groups in most crucial situations.
However, as the social interactions became more indi-
vidualized and interpersonal as with dating and marriage, Whites were least preferred, and Blacks and
other minority groups were more preferred.

328. Hunt, C. L. "Negro-white perceptions of interracial
housing." Journal of Social Issues, 15(4), 1959, 24-29.

The study was concerned with examining the effect on
property values and neighbor relations of integration
in housing in Kalamazoo, Michigan. Black families in
the area were interviewed along with the White neighbor
on either side, one White resident selected at random
across the street, and one White resident selected at
random in the next block. Some of the results were
that 65.2 percent of the Black respondents and 67.7
percent of the White sample said they liked living
in the neighborhood very much. Seven percent of the
Black subjects gave approval to living in a mixed
neighborhood, while only 20 percent of the White
respondents did. And when asked how people in the
neighborhood reacted to the entry of Blacks, 3 percent
of the Whites said they had been friendly, while 65
percent of the Blacks felt this way.

329. Hyman, H. H. and Sheatsley, P. B. "Attitudes toward
desegregation." Scientific American, 195(6), 1956, 35-39.

The authors discussed the 14-year sample made by the
National Opinion Research Center concerning the opinion
of the nation on segregation and integration. In the
1940's, regional differences were found to be sharp and
nearly everyone had an opinion. Additionally, those who
upheld segregation tended to be anti-integration concerning any aspect of the issue raised. But, in the
year of the article things had changed. In 1942, less
than one-third of those questioned favored school integration, while in the mid-1950's about half endorsed
the idea. In 1942, two-thirds were opposed to the idea
of living on the same block with a Black person; however, at the time of the present article a majority of
those asked did not object. Also, in the North, support
for school integration rose among Whites from 40 percent
in 1942 to 61 percent in the mid-1950's. The authors
commented that the "long-term trend" was in the direction

of integration, and they looked forward with interest to
the results of future opinion surveys in those areas.

330. Izard, C. E., Chappell, J. E., and Weaver, F. "Funda-
mental emotions involved in black-white encounters characterized by race prejudice." Proceedings of the American Psychological Association, 78th Annual Convention, 5, 1970, 357-
358.

The study attempted to measure the emotions involved in
a Black-White encounter characterized by racial prejudice. Black and White students at three universities in
Nashville, Tennessee, responded under varied conditions
to the Differential Emotion Scale. Black subjects were
asked to describe the emotions that characterized the
experience of being the recipient of race prejudice in
an imagined and in two remembered situations. White subjects were asked to predict how Blacks and prejudiced
Whites would feel in these encounters. White subjects
were also asked to estimate their degree of freedom from
personal, social, and cultural forces or pressures underlying race prejudice and made the same estimates for
their parents. At the time of the writing of the article,
the authors had completed only results for the Black subjects. These results confirmed the hypotheses and were
that the situation of the first encounter with prejudice
elicited higher scores on surprise, guilt, shyness, and
fear-distress on the Differential Emotion Scale. The
imaginary situation elicited higher scores on anger-
disgust-contempt than the actual situations. And, the
most recent encounter elicited a higher score on the
factor than did the first encounter.

331. Jaffee, C. L. and Whitacre, R. "An unobtrusive measure
of prejudice toward Negroes under differing duration of
speech." Psychological Reports, 27(3), 1970(Dec), 823-828.

The study investigated the relationship between the
voting behavior of White subjects toward a Black or
White individual in a group discussion when the Black
or the White individual talked more than anyone else in
the group or did not speak. The findings showed that
in the silent control condition there was no significant
difference in the subject's voting behavior for the
Black or White individual. However, in the high-talk
experimental condition, Blacks received fewer votes than
Whites.

332. Jefferson, R. B. "Some obstacles to racial integration." Journal of Negro Education, 26, 1957, 145-154.

Jefferson discussed some of the negative effects of
prejudice, discrimination, and segregation on Blacks as
well as Whites. He noted that although the Supreme
Court decision of May 17, 1954, concerning desegregation removed some of the legal barriers against

integration, there were other social barriers which were
effective in perpetuating discrimination and which subsequently affected the personalities of Blacks and Whites.

333. Jeffries, V. "Cultural values and antagonism toward
Negroes." Dissertation Abstracts, 29(2-A), 1968, 692-693.

Jeffries investigated the relationship between certain
cultural values and attitudes of solidarity and antagonism toward Blacks. Interviews were taken with Whites
from six communities in Los Angeles (integrated and all
White). The relationship between attitudes of solidarity
and antagonism and the cultural values "were explained in
terms of the integration of the ideological components of
cultural or personality systems."

334. Johnson, D. A., Porter, R. J., and Mateljan, P. "Racial
discrimination in apartment rentals." Journal of Applied
Social Psychology, 1(4), 1971(Oct), 364-377.

Minority groups perceived the lack of adequate housing
in a Southern California city as the result of racial
discrimination. To investigate this, apartment houses
were visited by male-female Black, White, and Mexican-
American couples. It was found that fewer apartments
were available to the Black and Mexican-American couples
than to the White couples. Blacks were quoted rents and
various fees which were higher than those quoted to
White couples. And, Black couples were discriminated
against most, Mexican-American couples next, and White
couples the least.

335. Johnson, G. B. "A sociologist looks at racial desegregation in the south." Social Forces, 33, 1954, 1-10.

Johnson predicted that change in the process of racial
desegregation would be gradual, not revolutionary. He
emphasized that gradualism should not be thought of as
a dirty word, but simply a useful and accurate description of the way social changes occur. The result of
the abandonment of compulsory segregation may rid the
South of the stigma of unfair legal compulsion against
Blacks and Blacks of a hated symbol of second-class
citizenship.

336. Johnson, J. T. "A study of counselor's galvanic skin
responses to video-taped stimuli of racial/sex pairings and
three verbal affect situations." Dissertation Abstracts
International, 33(7-A), 1973(Jan), 3293.

The experimenter investigated the galvanic skin response
and social acceptability ratings of White rehabilitation
counselors while they viewed video-taped presentations
of different pairings of Black and White, male and
female characters in three types of affective situations.
Subjects tended to react more to the affect being

portrayed than to the pairing of characters. Negative
reactions were found to occur with affectionate situations as opposed to neutral ones when mixed-race pairings were used. In general, the counselors did not
exhibit exceptionally negative attitudes toward Blacks
in most situations; however, four pairings produced the
greatest galvanic skin response measurements and the
lowest social acceptability ratings: Black male-White
female, White male-Black female, White female-Black
female, and White male-White female. Three pairings
were also found to have the lowest ratings: White male-
White male, Black female-Black female, and Black male-
Black female.

337. Johnson, S. and Johnson, D. W. "The effects of other's
actions, attitude similarity, and race on attraction toward
others." Human Relations, 25(2), 1972(Apr), 121-130.

Johnson and Johnson examined the effects of similarity
of attitudes, race, and goal facilitation or frustration
on attraction to a same- or other-race stranger in order
to clarify an effective approach to increasing attraction between Blacks and Whites. The results showed that
when the other person was perceived to have similar attitudes, he was more attractive than when he had dissimi-
lar attitudes, regardless of his race. Additionally,
expected cooperation from the other person rather than
consensual validation was found to account for much of
the relationship between similarity of attitudes and
attraction.

338. Jones, B. E., Lightfoot, O. B., Palmer, D., Wilderson,
R. G., and Williams, D. H. "Problems of black psychiatric
residents in white training institutes." American Journal
of Psychiatry, 127, 1970(Jul-Dec), 798-803.

The paper was an outgrowth of the training experiences
of five Black psychiatrists. They presented the conclusions they reached on the basis of experience in three
predominantly White psychoanalytically oriented training programs in the East and Midwest. Their thesis as
stated was that such schools were failing to produce
psychiatrists, Black or White, who were motivated or
prepared to address themselves to the mental health
needs of the Black community because of "White institutionalized racism." Some of the specific criticisms
were that (1) Blacks were expected to assimilate and
adopt the White middle-class values of the patients,
residents, or staff members around them. Their unique
or personal feelings were overlooked or misunderstood.
(2) Patients were selected who were believed to be
"good" and non-troublemakers who would benefit from
psychotherapy, and these were usually the middle-class
housewife, junior executive, or student. (3) Supervi-
sion of the programs was in the hands of White middle-
class psychiatrists whose training and background did

not provide them with the sensitivity for understanding
many of the problems of their Black patients or staff
members. Specific and general recommendations were made
regarding these areas.

339. Jones, J. P. "Negro stereotypes in children's literature: The case of Nancy Drew." Journal of Negro Education,
40, 1971, 121-125.

The author discussed the various negative stereotypes
attributed to Blacks in the Nancy Drew series of the
1930's and the contrastingly positive stereotypes given
to White characters.

340. Kaplan, P. E. and Fugate, D. "Pilot study of racial
interaction in a public place: Northern and southern settings compared." International Journal of Group Tensions,
2(3), 1972, 63-79.

Kaplan and Fugate studied the social manifestations of
racial interaction in supermarkets in northern and southern cities. It was found that patterns of racial contact differed for the two regions. In the South, avoidance was minimal because of the wide status gap which
allows for close but unequal contact. And, in the North,
avoidance was greatest because of the ambiguity governing interracial contact. Additionally, avoidance was
greater for males than for females, regardless of race.
(Summary of journal abstract.)

341. Karlins, M., Coffman, T., and Walters, G. "On the fading of social stereotypes: Studies in three generations of
college students." Journal of Personality and Social Psychology, 13, 1969, 1-16.

The objective of the study was to examine five aspects
of stereotyping by Princeton students over a 35-year
period: (1) changes in content, (2) changes in uniformity, (3) changes in favorableness of stereotypes,
(4) the relationship between uniformity and favorableness, and (5) differences between social stereotypes
of high school versus prep school graduates in the current population. The subjects were White undergraduates.
They were asked to select from a list of 84 adjectives
those they felt were typical of 10 racial-national
groups, in turn, including Blacks. Only results for
responses given the "Americans" and "Blacks" will be
presented. The subjects' characterization of Americans
in the present study was less flattering than in previous ones. Here the term used most often was materialistic. Industrious and intelligent were used by only 23
and 20 percent of the subjects, respectively. A more
favorable characterization over the 25-year period since
the Katz and Braly (1933) study was found for Blacks.
In the early study, the most frequently used traits for
Blacks were superstitious (84%) and lazy (75%). These

traits were attributed to Blacks by only 13 and 26 percent of the present subjects, respectively. The new
characterizations for Blacks were musical (47%), pleasure-loving (26%), ostentatious (25%), and happy-go-
lucky (27%).

342. Kassarjian, H. H.   "The Negro and American advertising,
1946-1965." Journal of Marketing Research, 6, 1969, 29-39.

The purpose of the study was to determine the frequency
with which Blacks appeared in mass circulation magazine
advertising; to determine the depiction of the Black's
role in print advertising; and to examine changes, either
in frequency or role that have occurred over the period
from 1946-1965. Three years were chosen for the study:
1946, 1956, and 1965. Results showed that 546 separate
ads containing Blacks were found in the almost 150,000
magazine pages investigated. This was less than one-
third of 1 percent of the total number of ads. In
regard to sex and age, it was found that more males and
adults appeared than females and children. The hypothesis, stating that the frequency of Blacks appearing in
magazine ads would be U-shaped over the three years
chosen for study, was confirmed. However, the frequency
of appearance of ads showing non-American Blacks tended
to increase. Occupational rate was found to change for
Blacks with more of them shown in higher status occupations in recent years. The occupational role of non-
American Blacks was not found to change since 1946. The
social role of Blacks and integrated advertisements with
Blacks and Whites shown as peers were found to increase.

343. Keesing's Research Report. Race Relations in the
U.S.A.: 1954-1968. New York: Charles Scribner's Sons,
1970, 280p.

The book documents the progress of race relations
between Blacks and Whites in the United States from
1954 to 1968. Some of the topics covered are: "Racial
Desegregation in Education, 1954-1957," "The Little
Rock Crisis, 1957-1959," "Measures to End Racial Segre-
gation in Public Amenities, 1954-1963," "The Civil
Rights Movement and Urban Riots, 1960-1965," and "The
Death of Martin Luther King."

344. Kennedy, J. L.   "Psychology and racism." New Scholar,
2(1), 1970(Apr), 136-150.

Kennedy explored the role of psychology in racial problems. Historical supports for racism were traced to
the beginning of the present century and subsequently
to the crystalization in the nature-nurture disputes.
Later research is seen as an elaboration of this conflict. It was suggested that modern psychology commit
itself to constructive social change, reach a larger
proportion of students, and adopt a more pragmatic
approach. (Summary of journal abstract.)

345. Kerckhoff, R. K.   "A study of racially changing neighborhoods."   Merrill-Palmer Quarterly, 14, 1957, 15-49.

   Kerckhoff studied the factors effecting the change of a
   Detroit neighborhood from an all White community to a
   mixed race one. He found that Whites justified selling
   their homes to Blacks by contending that no White pur-
   chaser could be found, that other White residence would
   soon be doing the same, and because Blacks would pay a
   higher price. Blacks denied any crusading motives,
   asserting that the homes were of nice quality and close
   to good schools and transportation. Whites who remained
   in the neighborhood did so out of loyalty to the area
   and the recognition that their homes were economical
   and comfortable.

346. Knapp, M. J. and Alston, J. P.   "White parental acceptance of varying degrees of school desegregation: 1965 and
1970."   Public Opinion Quarterly, 36(4), 1972-1973(Win),
585-591.

   The experimenters questioned under which conditions White
   parents would or would not object to sending their children to school with Black children: when Blacks were in
   the majority, when they were equal in number, or when
   they were in the minority. The article presented information indicating the degree of school integration
   acceptable during 1965 and 1970 in terms of region, sex,
   and age. Three questions designed to tap the attitudes
   of the parents were given by the Gallup Organization
   and were given to a representative sample of White
   Americans with one or more children in grade or high
   school. Results showed that parents in the South were
   more resistant to school integration in any form, irre-
   spective of the year the poll was taken. Non-southern
   parents objected (in 1965) to Blacks being at least half
   or a majority of the student population, and they maintained this attitude in 1970. The decline in regional
   differences from 1965 to 1970 was a result of southern
   parents becoming more liberal, while non-southern parents
   remained relatively constant. Parents in the South
   became more liberal toward integration, but no significant changes were indicated for either sex of parent in
   the North. Lastly, according to age effects, southern
   parents in 1970, who were over and under 40, objected
   to any form of school integration, and approximately the
   same proportion did not object. In the North, older parents were more resistant to integration than younger
   parents.

347. Koenig, F. W. and King, M. B.   "Cognitive simplicity
and outgroup stereotype."   Social Forces, 42(3), 1964, 324-
327.

   Koenig and King hypothesized that cognitive simplicity
   was positively related to outgroup stereotyping and

tested this prediction with the students at a church-
related university in the Southwest. Cognitive com-
plexity or simplicity was determined by the accuracy
with which each student perceived the attitudes of
others and by the similarity of their own attitudes
to the attitudes attributed to others. Measures of
stereotyping were used with Blacks as the stimulus
object. It was found that estimates of cognitive
simplicity were directly related to the measures of
stereotyping.

348. Kurokawa, M. "Mutual perceptions of racial images:
White, black, and Japanese-Americans." Journal of Social
Issues, 27(4), 1971, 213-235.

The mutual and self-percepts of the racial images of
Black, White, and Japanese-American college students,
school children, and adults were examined. College and
adult subjects were asked to choose five traits out of
84 to describe each racial group. The children were
asked to describe racial images in their own words. It
was found that there was only partial support for the
hypothesis that Whites would be given the most positive
traits and minority groups the negative traits. Whites
were described as materialistic and pleasure-loving;
Blacks as musical, aggressive, and straightforward; and
Japanese as industrious, ambitious, loyal to their
family, and quiet.

349. La Fargue, J. P. "Role of prejudice in rejection of
health care." Nursing Research, 21(1), 1972(Jan), 53-58.

La Fargue investigated possible racial prejudice in
White nurses and the reactions of Black patients in an
effort to determine whether prejudice kept Black patients
from seeking health care. She measured the racial attitudes of White nurses and interviewed Black families.
It was found that prejudice among the nurses was minimal;
however, Black families seemed to perceive prejudice in
the clinic nurses and in some health workers, but not
in public health nurses or nutritionists. (Summary of
journal abstract.)

350. Larson, R. F., Ahrenholz, G. L., and Grazyslene, L. R.
"Integration attitudes of college students at the University
of Alabama." Journal of Social Psychology, 63(2), 1964,
327-332.

The purpose of the study was to determine whether college students at the University of Alabama were willing
to accept integration. The responses of these students
were compared with those of students in Texas in 1952.
Some of the results were that the Alabama students were
less favorable toward integration than the Texas group.
Additionally, a somewhat discrepant finding was that
the image of Blacks was more favorable than the attitudes toward them.

351. Lee, F. F. "Social controls in the race relations pattern of a small New England town." Social Forces, 33, 1954, 36-40.

Lee was interested in the means used to control and perpetuate a race relations pattern in Branford, Connecticut, and the processes and techniques of social control which keep Blacks "in their place." Interviews, participant observations, and the perusal of documents were techniques used to obtain information about the social controls. The results showed that control operated in terms of status factors, the influence of mores on White citizens, dynamic actions by Whites against Blacks, and self-imposed segregation by Blacks. Lee suggested that the four of these controls be considered integral parts of the concept of social control.

352. Lees, H. "Negro neighbors." Atlantic Monthly, 197, 1956, 59-63.

Lees discussed some examples of Black families and Black individuals who are blocked from obtaining homes in White neighborhoods by rental agents and home owners who did not want to sell their homes to Blacks. There were a number of reactions such as residents who wanted to buy out a prospective Black home buyer or scare him away. Lees concluded with some helpful suggestions by the Commission on Human Relations for helping a changing neighborhood absorb the change relatively smoothly and painlessly.

353. Leibman, M. "The effects of sex and race norms on personal space." Environment and Behavior, 2, 1970, 208-246.

Leibman investigated the relationship between the race of another individual and two forms of spatial behavior --distance and intrusions. The subjects were females employed by the same company and in secretarial or editorial capacities. Four confederates were used--a Black and a White female and a Black and a White male. In one condition the subject was to choose a seat on a six-foot bench which was already occupied at one end by a confederate. This part of the experiment took place in a conference room. Distance between subject and confederate was measured by the experimenter. In an intrusion choice condition, the subject could choose between two benches occupied by a confederate, varying in race or sex. In the intrusion-non-intrusion condition, subjects were given a choice between an empty bench and one occupied by a White female confederate. Only White subjects participated here. The hypotheses were that White females would maintain greater interpersonal distances from male strangers than from females and from Black strangers than from White ones. Results showed that the subjects sat at similar distances from all four confederates. However, larger distances tended to occur in

relation to male confederates and smaller distances to
female confederates. For the intrusion condition, intrusion of personal space was avoided when possible. The
hypothesis predicting that females would be more likely
to choose to intrude upon another female rather than a
male was supported. However, a hypothesis concerning
intrusion preferences and race were not confirmed.

354. Lessing, E. and Zagorin, S. W. "Black power ideology
and college students' attitudes toward their own and other
racial groups: A correction." Journal of Personality and
Social Psychology, 22(3), 1972(Jun), 414-416.

The article presented a number of corrections of an earlier printing. The hypothesis predicting that subjects
high in Black power orientation would perceive a significantly smaller distance between Black person and Ideal
person and between Black person and Friend, than would
subjects low in this orientation, received full rather
than partial support among White subjects. The hypothesis predicting that subjects high in Black power orientation would perceive a significantly smaller distance
between White person and Enemy than subjects low on this
variable was upheld. Among the other changes was the
upholding of the hypothesis predicting that subjects low
in Black power ideology would produce a lower evaluative
factor score for Black person than for Negro person or
Colored person in the White sample. Additionally, a
restatement of the findings presented in the earlier
discussion section was made.

355. Levy, S. G. "Polarization in racial attitudes." Public
Opinion Quarterly, 36(2), 1972(Sum), 221-234.

The author was interested in identifying the subgroups
within the American population which differed greatly
from each other concerning attitudes toward race relations. The data came from two sources: a national survey of adults 18 or older for the Violence Commission in
1968, and a survey of adults 18 or older done in six
central cities in the North between 1966 and 1967.
Results from the commission survey showed that both
groups gave support to the idea that Blacks and Whites
should attend the same schools, and both were unlikely
to move if individuals of a different race moved next
door. However, there was a sharp decrease in similarity
of attitudes (with many Whites not endorsing the idea)
when the issue concerned housing and the alternative
became many individuals of a different race moving into
the neighborhood. Another finding was that the greatest
resistance to integration occurred among White subgroups
residing in the South. And Whites who were low in education and political activity were noticeably less integrationist. Lastly, high political activity coupled
with either high education or residence in the East were
the major factors in greater integrationist attitudes.

Results for cities showed no overlap in the scores of
the White and Black groups despite the fact that all of
the respondents were from the South. For education, low
education among Whites and Blacks was associated with
the fact that they were less in favor of integration.
Older Blacks and Whites were less in favor of integration than younger respondents. No distinction by sex
was found for White respondents, but White female
responses on a Riot Causes and Riot Prevention Scale
were closer to those of Black respondents.

356. Levy, S. G. "Polarized subgroup analysis of whites and
non-whites." Proceedings of the 77th Annual Convention of
the American Psychological Association, 4(Pt. 1), 1969,
301-302.

Levy used a procedure for identifying subgroups in the
population which maximally differed from each other to
examine attitudes on race relations obtained from 6,000
adults in six northern cities and 1,200 adults across
the nation. In the first sample, average subgroup
scores of Whites did not overlap those of non-White
subgroups; and in the second sample, only one overlapped
even though multiple discriminating variables to define
subgroups in each race were used. Race alone accounted
for almost all of the differences in attitude. Large
differences in race also appeared in political activity
and attitudes toward the Vietnam War. (Summary of
author abstract.)

357. Lieberson, S. and Fuguitt, G. V. "Negro-white occupational differences in the absence of discrimination."
American Journal of Sociology, 73(2), 1967, 188-200.

Lieberson and Fuguitt distinguished between two types
of handicaps faced by Blacks--discrimination which
involves rejection of Blacks simply because they are
Blacks and a handicap which occurs because Blacks occupy
an inferior position on variables which, although
racially neutral, operate to their disadvantage. They
used a Markov model to project future Black-White occupational patterns based on current analysis of father's
and son's occupation and education and the relationship
between the two. It was predicted that racial differences in occupation would decline sharply after only
one generation in which discrimination was absent; however, several generations would be needed before parity
was obtained.

358. Lief, H. I. and Stevenson, I. P. "Psychological
aspects of prejudice with special reference to desegregation." American Journal of Psychiatry, 114, 1958, 816-823.

Lief and Stevenson reviewed the knowledge of prejudice
as a problem in mental health from the following stand-
points: the nature of prejudice, factors promoting

prejudice, the influence of learning and education, and
the influence of group relations on prejudice. (Summary
of journal abstract.)

359. Lind, A. W. (Ed.)   Race Relations in World Perspective.
Honolulu: University of Hawaii Press, 1955, 488p.

Seventeen papers dealing with various aspects of race
relations are presented in the book by different authors.
Some of the topics include rigidity and fluidity in race
relations, social roles in race relations, adjustment
problems of Black and emigrant elites, and the Black
person in the United States. (Summary of journal
abstract.)

360. Linn, L. S. "Verbal attitudes and overt behavior: A
study of racial discrimination." Social Forces, 43(3),
1965, 353-364.

Linn attempted to measure the relationship between racial
attitudes and overt behavior among female college students. Each subject was asked to pose for a photograph
with a Black male after a measure of racial attitude had
been given. Linn found that there were discrepancies
between verbal attitudes and overt behavior which were
suggested to be a function of the level of social involvement with the attitude object as well as the amount of
prior experience with that person. It was concluded that
statements of racial behavior based solely on attitude
measurements may have little reliability unless validated
empirically first. (Summary of article abstract.)

361. Loiselle, R. H. and Williamson, L. T. "Perceptual
defense to racially significant stimuli." Perceptual and
Motor Skills, 23(3, Pt. 1), 1966, 730.

Loiselle and Williamson hypothesized that White female
college students would show perceptual defense to
racially critical stimuli significantly more than to
racially neutral stimuli. The critical stimuli were
color pictures of a Black man and woman, a Black man
and a White woman, and a White man and Black woman.
The neutral pictures were of a White man and woman.
Significant differences were found for the number of
exposures to recognition for critical and neutral pictures and for the galvanic skin response to the pictures. Additionally, after the students were divided
into an anti-Black and a pro-Black group and given a
card-sorting task, it was found that there was a significant difference between the groups in terms of the
number of exposures to recognition of the critical and
neutral pictures.

362. Long, B. H., Zeller, R. C., and Thompson, E. E. "A
comparison of prejudices: The effects of chronic illness,
old age, education, and race upon friendship ratings."
Journal of Social Psychology, 70(1), 1966, 101-109.

The study determined that age, health, race (Black or
White), and education significantly affected the friendship ratings of White college students. And, the order
of importance of the factors was health, education,
race, and age.

363. Lorenz, G. K. "Attitudes toward racial desegregation
among the blind, and patterns of concensus between blind and
sighted relatives." Dissertation Abstracts, 29(11-A), 1969,
4116.

Lorenz was concerned with attitudes toward racial desegregation among White blind adults as compared to sighted
relatives. It was hypothesized that the blind would be
like the sighted in their attitudes toward desegregation,
and the assumption was supported. Northern blind were
more inclined to favor desegregation than were southern
blind in similar ways as the sighted. In any subculture,
the blind were more inclined to favor desegregation than
the sighted; and this tendency increased with early onset
and long duration of blindness.

364. Mahan, T. W. and Mahan, A. "Urban to suburban school
bussing: The differential views of various segments of the
community after two years of success." Proceeding of the
77th Annual Convention of the American Psychological Association, 4(Pt. 2), 1969, 861-862.

Project Concern, an urban to suburban bussing program,
was met with a great deal of resistance, fear, and
vehemence. In June, 1968, it completed two years of
operation which had been called successful. However,
it was clear that studies of success would not be
enough to maintain it. Community support was necessary.
The expressed feelings and attitudes of ghetto parents,
suburban parents, citizens, and pupils were described
and analyzed in an attempt to sketch a natural history
for community change programs. (Summary of author
abstract.)

365. Mann, J. H. "The influence of racial group composition
on sociometric choices and perceptions." Journal of Social
Psychology, 48, 1958(Aug), 137-146.

The study was concerned with the influence racial group
composition of small leaderless groups had on friendship choices and perceptions of members. Black and
White individuals were used as subjects. Some of the
results were that (1) the friendship choices of Whites
were more similar to each other when they met in groups
in which they were in the majority than in equality
groups, (2) the friendship choices for Blacks showed
the reverse trend, (3) the friendship choices of Blacks
were more similar to each other when they were in the
minority position than when in the majority position,
and (4) the friendship choices of Whites were more

similar to Blacks when they were in a minority position
than when in the majority position.

366. Mann, J. H.   "The influence of racial prejudice on
sociometric choices and perceptions."   Sociometry, 21, 1958,
150-158.

Black and White graduate students were randomly assigned
to groups of six meeting in a leaderless group discussion four times a week for three weeks.   The subjects
were required to make friendship choices and to predict
the choices of other group members.   It was found that
the students tended to prefer friends of their own race,
that White students were more aware of the preferences
of members of their own race than were Black students,
that older Black students were more aware of the social
preferences of Whites than were older Whites of the
preferences of Blacks, and that older Whites preferred
Whites as friends more than older Black students preferred Blacks.   (Summary of journal abstract.)

367. Mann, J. H.   "The influence of racial prejudice on
sociometric status in interracial groups."   Psychological
Reports, 3, 1957, 585-588.

The aim of the study was to determine whether friendship
choices or popularity in an interracial group were
influenced by the racial prejudice of the members.   It
was predicted that there would be an inverse relationship between racial prejudice and popularity among the
members.   The findings showed that there was only slight
support for the hypothesis.

368. Marchionne, A. M. and Marcuse, F. L.   "Sensitization
and prejudice."   Journal of Abnormal and Social Psychology,
51, 1955, 637-640.

Slides were shown to two groups of subjects previously
selected for high and low ethnocentrism.   Half of the
subjects in each category were shown a slide of a Black
man attacking a White man with a knife, the other half
were shown a slide of a White man attacking a Black man
with a knife.   Recall measures of picture content were
taken.   The results showed that the superior recall
of the pictures attributed to those high in prejudice
(when congruous material was presented) was attributed
to sensitization.   (Summary of journal abstract.)

369. Martin, J. G.   "Racial ethnocentrism and judgment of
beauty."   Journal of Social Psychology, 63(1), 1964, 59-63.

The study was designed to answer the question, "What
is the relationship between racial group membership and
judgment of female beauty by males? . . ." from three
racial groups--Whites, Blacks, and Africans.   It was
hypothesized that the beauty judgments of Whites and

Blacks would show a high positive correlation, that the
beauty ratings of Whites would be more highly correlated
with independent rankings of females on a Black-White
racial scale than the rankings of the Blacks, and that
the rankings of Africans would be closer to those of
Blacks than Whites and that they would show some bias
toward the more Black females in their judgments. Subjects were shown 10 magazine photos of faces of Black
females. They were asked to arrange the pictures in
order of attractiveness. Additionally, 15 judges were
asked to rank the pictures from "most Negroid and least
Caucasian" to "least Negroid and most Caucasian."
Results showed that Whites and Blacks shared a common
esthetic standard for judging beauty and that White
features were considered to be more attractive than
Black features. There was also a moderately close
association between the ratings of the Black and White
subjects and the judges' ratings on a racial scale in
that both Blacks and Whites judged the more Black
females to be less attractive. The judgments of the
African subjects were found to be closer to those of
the White subjects than to those of the Black subjects.
However, the African subjects' judgments were less
highly correlated with the judges' racial ratings than
were those of the two American judges.

370. Marx, G. T.   "Protest and prejudice: The climate of
opinion in the Negro American community." Dissertation
Abstracts, 28(1-A), 1967, 310.

The study developed out of an interest in how response
to the civil rights struggle had affected the attitudes
of Blacks toward Whites. Marx used data from a non-
southern nationwide sample of Blacks in metropolitan
areas and special area samples from Atlanta, Birmingham, Chicago, and New York in an effort to analyze attitudes of protest and intolerance. Some of the findings
were that militancy was more prevalent among the young,
males, and individuals raised in the North and in urban
areas. Additionally, when attitudes toward White Jews
and toward Whites, in general, were sought, it was
found that attitudes toward Jews were more favorable
than those toward Whites.

371. Marx, G. T.   "The white Negro and the Negro white."
Phylon, 28(2), 1967, 168-177.

The paper was concerned with those who live with the
stigma of being Black and with some Whites who might
feel that "White is the color of evil." Both groups
are primarily identified with the values they reject--
Blacks because of their skin color and often their
lower-class background and beatniks because of the
white skin color and middle-class background. In
attempts to avoid identification with their past, they
try very hard to show that they are the opposite. As

a result of this, each may have misconceptions of what it really means to be middle class and White and what it means to be Black.

372. Masuoka, J. and Yokley, R. L. "Essential structural requisites in race relations." Social Forces, 33, 1954, 30-35.

Masuoka and Yokley asserted that the two theories that were used to explain race relations--the cycle of race relations and caste and class--were not incompatible and that the conflict between them was more apparent than real. Further in their paper, they discussed the concepts of race prejudice, social distance, role, and status and proposed them as the essential structural requisites in race relations.

373. Matthews, D. R. and Prothro, J. W. "Southern racial attitudes: Conflict, awareness, and political change." The Annals of the American Academy of Police and Social Science, 344, 1962(Nov), 108-121.

The aim of the study was to analyze racial attitudes among Black and White southerners by focusing on opinions about segregation. It also examined the prospects for attitude change and the awareness of the attitudes of members of the other race. Some results were that Whites strongly supported segregation, while Blacks supported integration just as heartily; and Blacks and Whites were incorrect in estimating each others' views toward segregation, although Whites were less correct than Blacks. Further discussion was given to the effects of education on feelings about segregation and to the prospects for change in White awareness about Blacks.

374. Mayovich, M. K. "Changes in racial stereotypes among college students." British Journal of Social Psychiatry and Community Health, 6(2), 1972, 126-133.

Mayovich examined the changes in stereotyped images of Blacks, Whites, and Japanese between 1932 and 1970. Black, White, and Japanese college students were asked to choose the five traits from a list of 84 which they felt were most characteristic of each racial group. The results showed that Blacks were considered to be aggressive and straightforward as compared with earlier stereotype studies in which they were given a primitive image. And Whites were then seen as materialistic and hedonistic (especially among Japanese subjects) as compared with their earlier image as progressive, individualistic, and intelligent.

375. Mayovich, M. K. "Stereotypes and racial images: White, black, and yellow." International Journal of Social Psychiatry, 18(4), 1972-1973(Win), 239-253.

Nine groups of Black, White, and Japanese-American subjects (composed of college students, adults, and fourth-
and fifth-graders) were asked to describe the traits of
Blacks, Whites, and Japanese-Americans. The adults and
college students were given an adjective check list from
which to make their choices; the children used their own
words. It was found that Whites were described as materialistic and pleasure-loving; Blacks were described as
musical, aggressive, and straightforward; and Japanese-
Americans were described as ambitious, industrious, loyal
to the family, and quiet. Changes in stereotypes for
these groups were demonstrated by comparing the results
with those of earlier studies. (Summary of journal
abstract.)

376. McDonagh, E. C. and Richards, E. S. Ethnic Relations
in the United States. New York: Appleton-Century-Crofts,
1953, 396p.

McDonagh and Richards analyzed ethnic relations in terms
of four aspects of status: social or interpersonal, educational, legal, and economic. The book is divided into
three parts: understanding, analyzing, and improving
ethnic relations. The ethnic groups considered are
Blacks, Jews, Mexicans, Indians, Japanese, Chinese, and
European immigrants. Research, programs for improving,
and trends in ethnic relations are also discussed.
(Summary of journal abstract.)

377. McEntire, D. "Government and racial discrimination in
housing." Journal of Social Issues, 13(4), 1957, 60-67.

McEntire noted that housing and the status of non-White
minority groups in the United States have a common history of governmental regulation. While the laws are very
specific in their pronouncement against discrimination
in housing, it is generally agreed that such discrimination is more stubborn and institutionalized and resistant
to change than any other kind. His paper discussed the
affects of various governmental laws regarding housing
discrimination.

378. McMillen, D. L. "Confidence in stereotypes concerning
ethnic groups." Journal of Social Psychology, 93(2), 1974
(Aug), 203-210.

McMillen was interested in determining the accuracy of
stereotypes toward Blacks and Whites. Black and White
male stimulus persons were presented to male undergraduates. One-half of the students were led to believe that
the experimenter had an independent check on the accuracy
of their ratings, while the other half were not. The
results showed that significant differences occurred
between the ratings of the Black and White persons only
when the students thought no check was available.

379. Meeland, T. and Berkun, M. "Sociometric effects of
race and combat performance." Sociometry, 21, 1958, 145-
149.

Immediately after combat in Korea, a sample of infantry-
men was formed into groups of 15 to 18 men having no
prior knowledge of one another. The men lived together
in groups behind the lines for a week of psychological
testing. They responded to a sociometric questionnaire
specifying four criteria for choosing and rejecting:
combat with you, leader in combat, share a bunker, and
rest and recreation. One of the results showed that
sociometric preferences were affected by race and characteristics associated with quality of combat performance. (Summary of journal abstract.)

380. Meer, B. and Freedman, E. "The impact of Negro neighbors on white home owners." Social Forces, 45(1), 1966,
11-19.

Meer and Freedman tested the prediction that equal-
status residential contact between Blacks and Whites
in a predominantly White middle- to upper-middle-class
neighborhood would lead to a reduction in prejudice.
Ten Black families were selected for study as well as
the 10 houses surrounding their homes. A control group
of surrounding families were chosen who lived three or
four blocks away from each Black family. The experimenters found that equal-status contact in housing did
lead to a reduction in prejudice; however, this change
did not necessarily generalize to other areas of interpersonal contact.

381. Middleton, R. "Racial problems and the recruitment of
academic staff at southern colleges and universities."
American Sociological Review, 26, 1961, 960-970.

Middleton conducted a survey in order to determine the
views of southern department chairman and doctoral candidates at leading universities toward racial problems
in the South. He found that many of the department
chairmen felt that the racial problems in their state
had had a detrimental effect on recruitment to the university in some degree. And, many doctoral candidates
refused to accept a teaching position in many of the
southern states thus further limiting the availability
of potential teachers. This limiting factor affects
the general qualitative level of southern faculties.

382. Montanye, T., Mulberry, R. F., and Hardy, K. R.
"Assessing prejudice toward Negroes at three universities
using the lost-letter technique." Psychological Reports,
29(2), 1971(Oct), 531-537.

A lost-letter technique was used to determine attitudes
toward Blacks at Brigham Young University as compared

to Arizona State University and the University of Cincinnati. Letters were placed with the address facing up in designated spots on the three campuses. Half of the letters bore a fictitious address for a medical research association, and the other half had the actual address of the "Negro Equal Rights Movement." It was found that Brigham Young students had the highest overall return rate, but that most of the letters were sent to the medical association. Arizona State students were the least responsive, but were relatively unaffected by prejudice. Lastly, Cincinnati students were like the Brigham Young students in terms of prejudice, but like the Arizona students in terms of responsibility.

383. Morgan, W. R. and Clark, T. N. "The causes of racial disorders: A grievance-level explanation." American Sociological Review, 38(5), 1973(Oct), 611-624.

Morgan and Clark presented three arguments which drew on data from a sample of 42 American cities. The data showed that frequency, precipitation conditions, and severity were important to the structure of racial disorders. Some of the conclusions were that cities with a greater confrontation probability (in terms of the number of Blacks and the number of police) had more frequent disorders; and cities with a high grievance level among Blacks had higher rates of disorder participation resulting in more severe disorders.

384. Moskos, C. C., Jr. "Racial integration in the armed forces." American Journal of Sociology, 72(2), 1966, 132-148.

In an article concerning the documentation of the degree of penetration and kind of distribution characterizing Black servicemen in the integrated army, interview and survey data were presented which dealt with solders' attitudes toward military desegregation. The responses of soldiers in two wars were compared--World War II and the Korean War. A shift in their attitudes toward integration was found in that a more positive disposition was noted among both Blacks and Whites in the latter war. Additional attitudes were obtained from Black soldiers in 1965 concerning which aspect of life was more egalitarian, and the majority felt that army life was more egalitarian than civilian life. However, southern Blacks had a more negative view of the Army than northern Blacks when comparing the two ways of life. When the reactions of White soldiers in both wars were looked at in terms of the amount of contact they had with Blacks, it was found that those who were in integrated settings preferred desegregation more than those who were in segregated settings.

385. Muir, D. E. "Through the school-house door: Trends in integration attitudes on a deep south campus during the

first decade of desegregation." Sociology and Social
Research, 58(2), 1974, 113-121.

The study was designed to investigate the changes in
attitude of White students toward Black students on the
University of Alabama campus over a 10-year period.
Four attitude surveys were administered at four different times--1963, 1966, 1968, and 1972. Likert-type
scales were administered. Results for attitudes concerning major areas of desegregation in 1963 showed that
less than a majority of those studied approved of sociable mixing or the desegregation of the university. With
later surveys, approving increased showing a trend
toward favorableness toward integration. In 1963, for
the responses to the social distance items, a majority
of the students did not object to only attending classes
with Blacks. However, by 1966, a majority were willing
to sit next to Black students in class. By 1969, interaction took on a sociable dimension (walking with Blacks
on campus and eating with them). In general, the trend
for the various types of attitudes studied concerning
Blacks was toward increasing acceptance. However, Blacks
were still rejected as roommates, social intimates, or
dates, although the social distance was decreasing.

386. Nemeth, C. and Sosis, R. H. "A simulated jury study:
Characteristics of the defendant and the jurors." Journal
of Social Psychology, 90(2), 1973(Aug), 221-229.

The experimenters studied two samples of subjects differing in class and political orientation in a simulated
jury situation. The defendant, accused of negligent
homocide, varied in race (Black or White) and attractiveness. Subjects were junior college students and college
students paid to participate. Four experimental conditions were used: male defendant, White, and attractive;
male defendant, Black, and attractive; male, White, unattractive; and male, Black, unattractive. Male and female
subjects were tested. Four different descriptions of the
defendant were used, depending upon the condition. Additionally, subjects were given a summary of facts concerning the case. Results showed that the sentence given was
significantly affected by attractiveness of the defendant
and background of the juror (college affiliation). The
unattractive defendant was sentenced more harshly than
the attractive ones, and the junior college sample gave
harsher sentences. Significant interactions were also
found between school and attractiveness of defendant and
school and race of defendant. Junior college subjects
gave harsher sentences to the unattractive defendants.
University subjects showed no significant difference
based on attractiveness and gave sentences similar to
those given by junior college subjects to attractive
defendants. With regard to race, neither sample discriminated when determining punishment. But, when the
defendant was White, junior college subjects gave a significantly harsher sentence than did university subjects.

387. Orbell, J. M. and Sherrill, K. S.   "Racial attitudes
and the metropolitan context: A structural analysis."
Public Opinion Quarterly, 33(1), 1969, 46-54.

The paper examined the impact on racial attitudes of
individual variables and aggregate variables alone and
then their impact when they were brought together. It
was suggested that individuals who have similar status
characteristics may respond differently when they live
in different parts of the city. Data were collected
from a study of Columbus, Ohio, in 1966. Responses to
questions were used to measure White racial attitudes.
Some of the results were that there was no significant
difference in hostility by the status variables used or
by any of the aggregate variables when treated in isolation. When looking at proximity to Blacks and area
status together, it was found that areas with high pro-
portions of Blacks were characterized by increasing
White hostility as status declined. However, Whites
living in areas that were without Blacks were more hostile when the areas had higher socioeconomic status.
Low socioeconomic status subjects living in low socioeconomic status areas were more hostile toward Blacks
than low socioeconomic status subjects living in high
socioeconomic status areas; however, subjects living in
the suburbs (high socioeconomic status subjects) tended
to be more hostile than those living in low socioeconomic
status areas.

388. O'Neile, J. E. A Catholic Case against Segregation.
New York: Macmillan, 1961, 155p.

The book contains seven chapters, written by different
authors, which discuss various aspects of prejudice,
discrimination, and their effects. Such topics as the
decisions of the Supreme Court from Plessy to Brown;
the development and philosophy of biracial schools; and
the psychological research showing that attitudes can
be modified, the adverse effect of segregation on personality, and the role of culture on intelligence test
scores are discussed.

389. Pearlin, L. I. "Shifting group attachments and attitudes toward Negroes." Social Forces, 33, 1954, 47-50.

The article reported some findings of a survey done
among students at a southern college for women concerning attitudes toward Blacks. Focus was upon the manner
in which the relationships of college students to various groups were correlated with attitudes toward Blacks.
The following hypotheses were presented: (1) Prejudice
would be related to the nature of the relationship that
the students maintained with groups of which they were
members before coming to college. The least prejudiced
subjects would be those with weak former ties, while
strongly prejudiced subjects would be those with strong

former ties. (2) Prejudice would be related to the
nature of the relationship students established since
coming to college. Part of the questionnaire concerned
their desire to see Blacks admitted to the school and
their willingness to participate with Black students in
several situations varying in degree of social distance.
Results showed that a change in attitude depended upon a
disattachment from groups from whom support for those
attitudes was derived; and the direction of the attitude
shift depended upon the norms of the groups to which new
attachments were developed.

390. Penner, L. "Interpersonal attraction toward a black
person as a function of value importance." Personality: An
International Journal, 2(2), 1971(Sum), 175-187.

Penner tested two hypotheses derived from Rokeach's theory of values and value change: the importance of the
value equality is correlated with the attitudes and
behavior a White person displays when he interacts with
a Black person, and changes in the importance of equality will be accompanied by changes in attitudes and
behavior in an interaction with a Black person. White
undergraduate controls ranked Rokeach's terminal values
twice at eight-week intervals. White experimental subjects ranked the terminal values, received a manipulation designed to increase the value equality in importance, and then ranked the values eight weeks later.
Three months later, experimental and control subjects
engaged in a conversation with a Black confederate, and
controls engaged in a conversation with a White confederate. Attitudinal and behavioral measures of attraction toward the confederates were given. For the group
with the Black confederate, perceived value similarity,
perceived behavior similarity, and eye contact indices
were significantly correlated with the importance of
the value equality. There were no significant correlations for the group with the White confederate. Students who received the value change procedure engaged
in significantly more eye contact toward the Black person than students not receiving this manipulation. The
results supported Rokeach's theory. (Summary of journal
abstract.)

391. Pettigrew, T. F. "Desegregation and its chances for
success: Northern and southern views." Social Forces, 35,
1957, 339-344.

Pettigrew noted that the mass media had kept the
nation's attention focused on race relations in the
South since the Supreme Court's 1954 decision abolishing racial segregation in public schools. However,
little notice had been taken of attitudes toward racial
integration in the North and how these attitudes might
compare with those of southerners. The study reported
was part of a larger one on regional differences in

intolerance toward Blacks. Attitudes concerning segregation were gathered in the North and South. The southern towns from which the sample was chosen were selected
to have Black populations varying from 10 to 45 percent.
The northern towns (all in New England) had less than 1
percent Blacks each. Two experienced interviewers conducted the inquiry. Results showed definite differences
between the two samples in regard to the ideas about
desegregation. By region, southerners were more against
segregation, discussed the issue with friends more, and
felt it was more important than northerners did. Concerning "degree of involvement," it was found that individuals of both regions favored segregation when it
involved them intimately but were less concerned about
it when it was more remote (as in mixed musical bands,
for example). Another finding was that the greater the
degree of authoritarianism, the more anti-Black and pro-
segregation was the subject in the North and South.
Lastly, for the southern subjects, the proportion of
Blacks living in a particular community was of crucial
significance in desegregation attitudes. High density
areas were more in favor of segregation and more pessi-
mistic about desegregation being accepted in the South
than were low-density areas.

392. Picher, O. L. "Attraction toward Negroes as a function of prejudice, emotional arousal, and the sex of the
Negro." Dissertation Abstracts, 27(2-B), 1966, 612.

Picher tested the hypothesis that if the social-sexual
taboo that White women should not interact socially with
Black men was effective, White women would be less
attracted to Black men than to Black women. The results
showed that highly prejudiced males and females were less
attracted to Black strangers than were low-prejudiced
subjects. Males generally disliked female Blacks more
than Black males, while female subjects showed no preference. And, highly prejudiced females were more
attracted to Black males than to Black females.

393. Pinkney, A. "The quantitative factor in prejudice."
Sociology and Social Research, 47(2), 1963, 161-168.

The purpose of the paper was to examine the extent to
which the number of minority group members affects the
attitudes of the dominant group toward them. The study
was done in a place in California which had varying pro-
portions of minority groups (Mexican-Americans, Blacks,
Chinese-Americans, Jews, Japanese-Americans, and
Indians). The data were collected from interviews with
random samples of White American adults. The article
dealt with one of the questions posed in the interview,
"Do you think you would ever find it a little distaste-
ful to go to a party and find that most of the people
are . . . ?" with the particular minority group filled
in. The results showed that the proportion of a

minority in the population was not necessarily consistently related to the amount of prejudice directed toward its members. Mexican-Americans and Blacks made up the largest groups, 10 and 8 percent, respectively; however, despite their difference in size, greatest hostility was directed toward Blacks. Similar data from other cities in different geographical locations lent support to these results in that in New York, for instance, where the population of minorities was 5 percent Italian-American, 3 percent Jews, and 2 percent Blacks, the interview question led to the most negative reactions toward Blacks. The experimenter suggested that racism appeared to be a function of visibility with those with the darkest skin receiving the greatest amount of prejudicial responses.

394. Platt, G. M. "Identification, prejudice, and selective memory." Dissertation Abstracts, 25(2), 1964, 1383.

A sample of Black individuals was tested as to degree of Black identification and degree of prejudice. The experimenter was interested in the effects of Black identification and prejudice on recall in a story rewriting task. The results showed that highly prejudiced individuals appeared to recall less, regardless of whether the content was stereotyped, anti-stereotyped, or neutral. And Blacks who identified with their own race were less able to recall stereotypes regarding the Black character than those who identified less with Blacks.

395. Polite, C. K. "Black self-hate in fraternity and sorority affiliates and in independent undergraduates at Michigan State University." Unpublished Master's thesis, Michigan State University, 1972.

The study was done to investigate the status of self-hate among Black undergraduates. Among various hypotheses it was predicted that because of the Black pride movement an unfavorable image of Blacks by Black undergraduates would not exist. It was also predicted that there would be a positive correlation between satisfaction with self and the evaluation of one's ethnic group. A sample of Black independent undergraduates and a sample of Black fraternity and sorority members were studied using a form of the semantic differential. The concepts evaluated were: "Me," "Negro," "Blacks," "White Protestant," and "Ideal Self." The bipolar adjectives were "intelligent-unintelligent," "clean-dirty," "industrious-lazy," "cultured-uncultured," "responsible-irresponsible," "good-bad," "strong-weak," and "active-passive." Results concerning the first hypothesis above were that the subjects evaluated Blacks more positively than White Protestants. Additionally, there was no relationship between the way the subjects evaluated Blacks and the way in which they evaluated White Protestants. Results for the second

hypothesis were significant indicating that a relationship did exist between evaluations of Me and Blacks.

396. Prentice, N. M. "The influence of ethnic attitudes on
reasoning about ethnic groups." Journal of Abnormal and
Social Psychology, 55, 1957, 270-272.

The study examined the relationships between ethnic attitudes and objective reasoning about ethnic groups. It
was predicted that tolerant subjects would bias their
reasoning in a favorable direction, while intolerant
subjects would bias their reasoning in an unfavorable
direction. The results showed that tolerant subjects
biased their reasoning in favor of ethnic groups; however, intolerant subjects did not bias their reasoning
against these groups. Prentice suggested that the
latter results may have been related to the fact that
there were no strongly prejudiced individuals in the
subject sample.

397. Preu, J. (Ed.) The Negro in American Society. Tallahassee, Florida: Florida State University, 1958, 89p.

The collection of papers consisted of the comments of a
group of social scientists on the Black person in America. Three chapters were concerned with the anthropological and economic views of Myrdal and Sumner in
relation to segregation and desegregation. The other
four chapters were concerned with the psychological
characteristics and the place of Blacks in southern
agriculture, politics, and the literature of American
history. (Summary of journal abstract.)

398. Proenza, L. and Strickland, B. R. "A study of prejudice in Negro and white college students." Journal of Social
Psychology 67(2), 1965, 273-281.

The study was done to document intensity of prejudice
among southern and northern college students and to examine significant methods of assessing prejudice. Black
and White undergraduates were subjects. A modified form
of the Bogardus Social Distance Scale and semantic differential ratings for the concepts "Negro," "White," "integration," and "segregation" were obtained. Results indicated that Blacks showed significantly less social
distance toward Whites than southern Whites exhibited
toward Blacks. No significant differences were found
between northern and southern males on the social distance scale, but White females in the North showed significantly less social distance toward Blacks than did
White females in the South. No significant difference
was found between semantic differential ratings of the
four concepts among White students in the North and
South. However, significant differences between races
were found for "Negro," "segregation," and "integration"
with Black students being more favorable toward the

first and last concepts and less favorable toward the
second than were Whites. In addition, Blacks were more
favorable toward the concept White than were Whites
toward Negro. No significant differences were found
between sexes, but significant interactions of sex and
race were found for Negro and White. In determining
the relationship between the social distance scale and
the semantic differential, a positive correlation was
found for ratings of segregation and a negative one for
integration. No correlations were found for Negro and
White.

399. Pugh, R. W. Psychology and the Black Experience.
Monterey, California: Brooks/Cole Publishing Co., 1972,
118p.

The book grew out of a symposium of Black psychologists
which was sponsored by the Department of Psychology of
Loyola University in 1970. These psychologists felt the
need to examine the significance of Black activism, the
nature of the Black experience, and some aspects of a
relationship professional psychology might have to these
factors. Part one of the book concerns a psychological
assessment of the Black Revolution and an examination of
Black student activism. Part two concerns the professional concerns of two Black clinical psychologists.
Finally, part three contains autobiographical recollec-
tions from the lives of two Black professional psychologists.

400. Rafky, D. M. "Police race attitudes and labeling."
Journal of Police Science and Administration, 1(1), 1973
(Mar), 65-86.

Rafky was interested in examining the meaning and use of
racial labels among urban police. He wanted to know
what labels police use to refer to Black Americans,
how police feel about Blacks and the significance of
their attitudes, whether the attitudes of police differ
from those of White in general and Whites in the same
economic and social position, whether labels are valid
indicators of racial attitudes, and how the relationship
between attitudes and labels vary among different subgroups of policemen. Questionnaires were given to a
sample of police and results of a recent opinion poll
were compared with these responses in order to compare
the attitudes of the police with those of other Americans. It was found that the police and Blacks preferred
the term "Negro." The term "Colored" was second in
popularity. The term "Black" was third choice among
both groups. Additionally, police were less ambivalent
than other groups, sticking to one label. Finally, it
was found that police were not more prejudiced than
the general public and that there was a relationship
between labeling and racial attitudes.

401. Ragland, G. R., Jr. "Attitudes of a selected group of Negro college students toward desegregated schools." Journal of Human Relations, 4(2), 1956, 103-110.

The study was done to determine what attitudes a selected group of Black college students had toward desegregated schools and to determine to what extent these attitudes were related to sex, farm, and non-farm backgrounds, anticipated vocation, academic standing in class, and leadership in outside activities. Graduating seniors at a four-year college were subjects. A questionnaire was administered to secure biographical data, anticipated vocation, desegregation attitudes, and the effect of desegregated schools on employment. Cumulative grade-point averages for each subject were also obtained. Some of the results were that in response to the question concerning their preference for attending separate but equal or mixed schools, 52 percent of the subjects preferred the segregated school: females more than males, teachers more than non-teachers, officers of clubs more than non-officers, and those with lower averages more than those with higher averages. In response to the question concerning separate but unequal schools, 23 percent favored segregation: farm subjects more than non-farm subjects, females more than males, teachers more than non-teachers, non-officers more than officers, and upper percentile more than lower. Lastly, in response to a question concerning letting their children go to a Black school or a mixed school, 11 percent favored the all Black school: females more than males and non-officers more than officers.

402. Rambo, W. W. "Own attitude and the aberrant placement of socially relevant items on an equal appearing interval scale." Journal of Social Psychology, 79(2), 1969, 163-170.

Statements expressing attitudes toward Blacks were scaled by groups of subjects who differed in own-attitude positions. Additionally, two different sets of instructions were used: one placed emphasis on the necessity for the subject to maintain a judgmental attitude; the other did not emphasize this. Results suggested that negative own-attitude subjects distributed judgments over a narrower segment of the scale and produced more inversions of statements than the other own-attitude groups. (Summary of author abstract.)

403. Rankin, R. E. and Campbell, D. T. "Galvanic skin response to Negro and white experimenters." Journal of Abnormal and Social Psychology, 51, 1955, 30-33.

The study reported an experiment showing a differential galvanic skin response on the part of White male college students to incidental contacts by Black and White experimenters. Subjects were told that they were participating in a word-association test during which their

galvanic skin response to the words would be recorded.
During the course of the experiment, a Black or White
experimenter alternately made incidental hand contact
with the subject as he purportedly adjusted dummy electrodes on the subject's left hand. The actual electrodes
were attached to the right hand. Results showed a highly
significant differential response to the two experimenters, with the greater response occurring toward the Black
experimenter. However, according to the author, while
this response may be logically interpreted as a response
to race, it was arbitrarily made since the two experimenters differed in size, height, and age, in addition to
skin color.

404. Ransford, H. E. "Blue-collar anger: Reactions to student and black protest." American Sociological Review, 37
(3), 1972(Jun), 333-346.

Ransford tested the prediction that working-class individuals would be antagonistic toward student movements
and Blacks using a sample of Los Angeles, California,
residents. He found that his hypothesis was confirmed
in that the subjects expressed punitive attitudes toward
student demonstrators, opposed giving more power to students, and felt that Blacks were pushing too hard for
things they did not deserve.

405. Ransford, H. E. "Skin color, life chances, and anti-
white attitudes." Social Problems, 18(2), 1970(Fal), 164-
179.

The study was done in Los Angeles, California, after the
Watts riot in order to determine the sources of White
antagonism in a situation of strongly felt and freely
expressed emotion. Of the Black males interviewed, dark-
skinned Blacks were lower in occupational and income
positions than light-skinned Blacks, suggesting that
skin color per se structures opportunity, regardless of
educational level. Dark-skinned Blacks expressed more
anti-White sentiments than light Blacks. Ransford
noted that color is only a strong predictor of anti-
White feelings among lower-class and working individuals, those with no social contact with Whites, and
those who feel powerless to exert control through
institutional channels.

406. Record, W. "Community and racial factors in intellectual roles." Sociology and Social Research, 41, 1956, 33-
38.

Record discussed the fact that there were pressures on
Black intellectuals to be concerned with social action
programs related to racial discrimination rather than
other areas of social reform. The intellectual who concerns himself with general domestic issues may be
viewed as neglecting his race in exchange for more

favorable prominence in the White world. The Black
intellectual cannot find a rewarding position in the
business world. However, he is free to participate or
not in social movements which are directed at changing
that order. The Black intellectual is rejected by the
dominant White order and lacks the freedom of movement
against the general forces which shape the larger social
structure. The effects of these two pressures on the
Black intellectual result in his continuing involvement
in efforts to redress the racial balance.

407. Redish, A. and Weissbach, T. A.   "Traits attributed by
white students to black fellow students versus blacks in
general." Journal of Social Psychology, 92(1), 1974(Feb),
147-148.

The experimenters hypothesized that when given the opportunity, White college students would choose not to
attribute a set of traits as especially characteristic
of Blacks and that the students would be more willing to
make trait attributions to a known subgroup of Blacks as
opposed to Blacks in general. Two groups of students
rated a set of 12 trait-descriptive adjectives. One
group rated Blacks in general and the other rated Blacks
at the college. The results were that both hypotheses
were supported and that when attributions were made,
they tended to be unfavorable. (Summary of journal
abstract.)

408. Richards, E. S.   "Attitudes of college students in the
southwest toward ethnic groups in the United States."
Sociology and Social Research, 35(1), 1950, 22-30.

The purpose of the study was to discover some of the
attitudes toward ethnic groups in the United States
which predominate among White college students in the
Southwest, to show the extent to which these attitudes
were positive or negative, and to determine the relative importance of several possible sources of ethnic
attitudes among college students. A multiple-choice
questionnaire referring to nine major ethnic groups was
administered to subjects who were instructed to check
the statements they felt were characteristic of the
ethnic groups. Results showed that many of the common
stereotypes were accepted by these students such that
Blacks were felt to act inferior to other people, would
steal, possessed a low moral standard, and were superstitious. For Mexicans, Blacks, and Japanese, the
majority of the statements were negative. When the
experimenter examined the sources of information for
these attitudes, he found that least scientific sources
were ranked in the highest positions, while the more
scientific sources were in the lowest positions.

409. Richards, S. A.   "The effects of the supervisor's race
upon his performance ratings and the group interaction in a

simulated organization." Dissertation Abstracts International, 31(5-B), 1970(Nov), 3049.

Richards investigated the effects of a supervisor's race upon his performance ratings and the group interaction in a simulated organization using male college students as subjects and as subject-supervisors. Some of the results showed that Blacks performed poorer than Whites in the role as superiors on certain skill dimensions. There was no significant difference in the behavior of subordinates supervised by Blacks and Whites. Subordinates with Black supervisors spoke more than those with White supervisors. And, in general, racial attitudes did not effect the performance ratings of the Black supervisors.

410. Roberts, H. W. "Prior-service attitudes toward whites of 219 Negro veterans." Journal of Negro Education, 22, 1953, 455-465.

The study was a report on the analysis of a group of papers written by a sample of Black veterans attending two colleges in Virginia. The purpose of the papers was to get an idea of their personal experiences and their reactions to them. The sample was divided into three groups based upon place of birth and rearing--two groups came from the South, the other from the North. The analysis showed that 75 percent had entered the service with negative attitudes toward Whites. When described by place of birth and rearing, it was found that 84.6 percent of those born in Virginia, 80 percent of those born in other southern states, and 30.8 percent of those born in the North entered the service with negative attitudes toward Whites. The experimenter sought reasons from the men concerning their attitudes and the five most repeated reasons were: (1) segregation and discrimination, (2) superiority attitudes of Whites, (3) the belief that Whites block Blacks' progress, (4) personal difficulties with Whites, and (5) seeing injustices done to Blacks. An examination of these reasons was made with respect to place of birth and rearing, and it was found that the same reasons prevailed and were most prevalent in those who came from other southern states, less prevalent in Virginians, and least prevalent in northerners. Positive attitudes were also found, and the reasons for these included social intercourse and reciprocity, living in mixed neighborhoods, attending mixed schools, participating in mixed school activities, attending mixed parties and picnics, playing together, visiting homes, and mixed dates. Some subjects were also found to have dual attitudes.

411. Robin, S. S. and Story, F. "Ideological consistency of college students: The bill of rights and attitudes towards minority groups." Sociology and Social Research, 48(2), 1964, 187-196.

Robin and Story attempted to determine the association
between belief in the bill of rights and attitudes toward
minorities among those who were not necessarily bound to
formal statements of ideology--college students. A scale
designed to measure agreement with the bill of rights and
one designed to measure attitudes toward minority groups
were administered. It was found that the students as a
whole agreed with the bill of rights and had favorable
attitudes toward minority groups. The correlation
between these two attitudes was significant and positive.

412. Rose, A. M. "Intergroup relations versus prejudice:
Pertinent theory for the study of social change." Social
Problems, 4, 1956, 173-176.

Rose pointed out that the laws of change governing intergroup relations are largely sociogenic, while those governing prejudice are psychogenic. Therefore, the study
of race relations, theories, and lines of research should
be determined by the nature of the problem. It may call
for a specific or interdiscriplinary approach. (Summary
of journal abstract.)

413. Rose, A. M., Atelsek, R. J., and McDonald, L. R. "Neighborhood reaction to isolated Negro residents: An alternative
to invasion and succession." American Sociological Review,
18, 1953(Oct), 497-507.

The study investigated the reaction of White neighbors
in a Minneapolis community toward the residency of a
Black family. Interviews were conducted in eight communities. The results indicated that Whites tended to
accommodate the Black family as a neighbor and that
those Whites who lived closer to the family had more
contact with them, had lived in the interracial situation for at least 10 years, and had a larger invest-
ment in the community were more favorable toward them
than were the other Whites.

414. Safier, A. "Dual minority status. Group identification and membership conflict: A study of black Jews."
Dissertation Abstracts International, 32(4-A), 1971(Oct),
2195-2196.

Safier studied the dual minority concept by investigating the attitudes of Black Jews with reference to (1)
their opinions about the ascribed and voluntary minority
groups, (2) the group they identify with the most, and
(3) the group they would choose if such a choice were
required. White Jews, Black Protestants, and the Black
Jews were asked to rate Jewish Americans, Black Americans, White Americans, and some other foreign-born individuals. The results indicated that the Black Jews were
in a state of incongruity. They rated Black Americans
negatively, but Jewish Americans positively. Safier
noted that the findings showed that these Dual Minority

members tended to identify more closely with the higher
esteem, voluntary membership group.

415. Sattler, J. M., Skenderian, D., and Passen, A. J.
"Examiners' race and subjects' responses to an attitude
scale." Journal of Social Psychology, 87(2), 1972(Aug),
321-322.

The purpose of the study was to determine whether an
examiner's race, a subject's anonymity, and his need
for approval affect the responses he gives on a paper-
and-pencil measure of attitudes toward Blacks. White
male and female college students were subjects. The
examiners were Black and White college students. The
results showed that in contradiction to the prediction,
the most favorable responses did not occur with a Black
examiner under non-anonymity, and with high need for
approval subjects.

416. Schlinger, M. J. and Plummer, J. T. "Advertising in
black and white." Journal of Marketing Research, 9(2),
1972(Mar), 149-153.

Schlinger and Plummer reported the responses of Black
and White women to all Black and all White casts in a
television commercial. The results showed no evidence
that Black middle-class consumers react negatively to
Black actors or that the substitution of Black for White
models has much effect on the responses of White consumers. (Summary of journal abstract.)

417. Schracy, F. J. "Measuring basic community attitudes:
A research project on Negro-white relationships in Springfield, Ohio." Sociology and Social Research, 35, 1951,
338-345.

The purpose of the study was to determine how individuals in Springfield, Ohio, measured on an attitude-
behavior questionnaire concerning Black-White relationships and to discover whether the racial attitudes could
be changed through workshops or human relations. A com-
bination of measures were planned to be used including
the Bogardus Social Distance Scale and the Grice-Remmers
studies. No results were reported since the paper was a
presentation of future plans.

418. Searles, R. and Williams, J. A., Jr. "Negro college
students' participation in sit-ins." Social Forces, 40(3),
1962, 215-220.

The questionnaire study found that the sit-in protests
of Black college students from three schools in North
Carolina were more indicative of their identification
with White middle-class values than they were an indication of social alienation.

419. Secord, P. F., Bevan, W., and Katz, B. "The Negro stereotype and perceptual accentuation." Journal of Abnormal
and Social Psychology, 53, 1956, 78-83.

Fifteen photographs, 10 of Black faces and five of White
faces, were rated by judges on two seven-point scales.
One scale included physiognomic traits, the other
included personality traits generally accepted as stereotypes of Blacks. Prejudice scores were also obtained
for the subjects. Results showed that there was no
decrease in stereotyping in moving from the most characteristic looking Black to the least; anti-Black judges
exaggerated the personality stereotype of Blacks, while
pro-Black judges deemphasized it; and both anti-Black
and pro-Black judges perceived the Black person as having more characteristic physiognomic traits than neutral
judges.

420. Sedlacek, W. E. and Brooks, G. C. "Race of experimenter
in racial attitude measurement." Psychological Reports, 30
(3), 1972, 771-774.

The Situational Attitude Scale was administered to two
groups of White undergraduates. One group was given the
scale by seven Black experimenters and the other was
given the scale by seven White experimenters. The
results showed no measurable effects due to the race of
the experimenter, and White students generally responded
negatively to Blacks in personal or social situations.
(Summary of journal abstract.)

421. Sedlacek, W. E., Brooks, G. C., and Mindus, L. A.
"Social attitudes of white university students and their
parents." Journal of College Student Personnel, 14(6),
1973(Nov), 517-520.

Sedlacek et al. administered the Sedlacek and Brooks
Situational Attitude Scale, which is a measure of attitudes toward Blacks, to incoming White freshmen and their
parents. This scale contains various personal and
social situations which are designed to evoke a racial
response on semantic differential scales. The results
indicated that the students and parents had negative
attitudes toward Blacks but that parents were more negative than students in rating situations concerning
rape, being stopped by a police officer, standing on a
bus, and magazine salesmen. (Summary of journal
abstract.)

422. Selltiz, C. and Cook, S. W. "Racial attitude as a
determinant of judgments of plausibility." Journal of
Social Psychology, 70(1), 1966, 139-147.

The study explored the possibility that ratings of
plausibility might serve as indirect measures of racial
attitudes. White college students were subjects and

were chosen from certain organizations which were expected
to hold certain attitudes about race relations. The subjects came from civil rights groups, courses in intergroup relations or minority group problems, and right-
wing political organizations and selected fraternities.
Results showed that on the self-description attitude
measure, students in militant civil rights organizations
were most unprejudiced, those in race relations classes
were next, and those in the political organizations and
specific fraternities were most prejudiced. On the
plausibility measure, subjects in the civil rights groups
felt pro-integration arguments were most plausible and
pro-segregation arguments least plausible. Those in the
political organizations and fraternities showed the
reverse.

423. Selltiz, C., Edrich, H., and Cook, S. W. "Ratings of
favorableness of statements about a social group as an indi-
cator of attitude toward the group." Journal of Personality
and Social Psychology, 2(3), 1965, 408-415.

Studies reporting that judgments of the favorableness of
statements about an attitude object are influenced by a
judge's attitudes toward the object have suggested that
such ratings might be used as a disguised measure of
attitude statements about Blacks. Attitude statements
were administered to groups of college students differing in attitude toward Blacks. It was found that scale
values assigned to statements by judges with different
attitudes were significantly different. And, difference
in ratings of unfavorable and intermediate statements
were systematic, with pro-integration students rating
them as more unfavorable.

424. Shuey, A. M., King, N., and Griffith, B. "Stereotyping
of Negroes and whites: An analysis of magazine pictures."
Public Opinion Quarterly, 17, 1953, 281-287.

The purpose of the study was to determine whether or not
Blacks and Whites were portrayed differently in magazine
pictures. The first two issues from each month in 1949
and 1950 of Life, The Saturday Evening Post, Time, and
The New Yorker were examined in addition to all issues
of Ladies' Home Journal during the two years and all
issues of Colliers in 1950 and the first two issues of
this magazine for each month of 1949. Pictures were
classified according to size, type (advertising or
non-ad), and occupational status of models (above
skilled, skilled-clerical, and below skilled). Because
it was difficult to determine the occupational status
of some individuals pictured, a heading titled unclas-
sified advertisement was made. It was found that Blacks
appeared much less frequently than Whites, and of the
pictures of Blacks that were found only a small percentage (4.6%) could be identified with the highest of the
three occupational categories. On the other hand,

69.95 percent of the Whites could be placed in the highest occupational category. Those Whites classified in
the highest occupational category were also shown enjoy-
ing more leisure and entertainment activities than Blacks
in the same category. No Blacks were pictured as skilled
or clerical workers, while 5.78 percent of the total number of pictures of Whites showed them in this category.
And, concerning the below-skilled category, 8.09 percent
of the pictures of Whites were such, while 95.24 percent
of the Blacks were depicted in this category. The experimenters also examined to what extent the ads reflected
actual occupational levels of Blacks and Whites and
found that although 9 percent of Blacks were actually
employed above semi- and unskilled jobs, less than 5 percent of the ads showed this. And, although 91 percent
were actually employed in the lowest jobs, 95 percent of
the ads showed them in this group.

425. Siegel, J. M. "A brief review of the effects of race
in clinical service interactions." American Journal of
Orthopsychiatry, 44(4), 1974, 555-562.

The paper contained a brief review of the literature
dealing with the role of race in clinical service interactions and placed special emphasis upon the Black
patient and the White clinician. It was concluded that
little firm evidence could be found concerning the
effects of race in such areas as psychological testing
and psychotherapy and counseling to suggest that Black
patients did better with a Black rather than a White
clinician.

426. Sigall, H. and Page, R. "Current stereotypes: A little
fading, a little faking." Journal of Personality and Social
Psychology, 18(2), 1971, 247-255.

The experimenters used a technique which was a version
of the "bogus pipeline" described by Jones and Sigall.
In this procedure, the experimenter claims to have access
to the subject's covert reactions by a machine which
provides a direct physiological measure of his attitudes,
and the procedure is designed to encourage the subject to
respond honestly. The method was used to get subjects to
present less socially desirable stereotypes than would
occur in a more typical rating scale situation where they
would be free to distort their responses. White male
undergraduates were subjects. A dummy machine called an
adapted electromyograph was used to convince the subjects
that a physiological measurement technique could tap their
actual attitudes. Stereotypic ratings showed that "Americans" were rated as being more talkative, conventional,
progressive, practical, intelligent, pleasure-loving,
industrious, ambitious, aggressive, and materialistic.
"Blacks" were rated as more musical, ignorant, and physically dirty.

427. Silberman, C. E. Crisis in Black and White. New York:
Vintage Books, 1964, 370p.

The book addressed itself to the problem of race relations in the United States with an introduction stress-
ing the fact that something had to be done immediately
to solve this problem and that nothing short of "a
radical reconstruction of American society [was]
required (p. 10)" if Blacks were going to take their
rightful place within the mainstream of this culture.

428. Simpson, G. E. and Yinger, J. M. Racial and Cultural
Minorities: An Analysis of Prejudice and Discrimination.
Rev. ed. New York: Harper, 1958, 881p.

In this revised edition, desegregation in education,
the causes of prejudice, and efforts to reduce discrimination were stressed. In part one, the types of major-
ity-minority situations, the mystical, administrative,
and biological approaches to race, the personality functions of prejudice, the role of culture in perpetuating
prejudice, the effects on victims, the types of adjustment, the effects on the bigot, and the sociology and
social psychology of anti-Semitism were discussed.
Parts two and three discussed various other factors
accompanying prejudice and suggested strategies for
changing prejudice. (Summary of journal abstract.)

429. Smith, B., Jr. "The differential residential segregation of working-class Negroes in New Haven." American
Sociological Review, 24, 1959(Aug), 529-533.

Smith focused on factors of behavior and attitudes of
segregated and unsegregated Blacks which may help to
explain differential segregation in housing. Subjects
were chosen from the former tenant files of the seven
local public housing projects in which the individuals
lived. No significant differences were found between
the segregated and nonsegregated groups in terms of
such factors as age, occupation, education, mobility
class position, skin color, personal appearance, or
speech. The factors which stood out in the out-moving
group were either directly or indirectly activities
which were useful in getting housing or attitudes about
what traits a home should or should not have.

430. Smythe, H. H. "Desegregation: The myth of 'good race
relations.'" Journal of Human Relations, 44, 1956, 61-65.

The writer noted that no aspect of the desegregation
issue had received more attention and widespread pub-
licity than the fallacy concerning the myth of good race
relations between Blacks and Whites in the South prior
to the difficulties which stemmed from the Supreme Court's
decision on school desegregation and that the assumption
indicated a dangerous ignorance of the real opinions and

attitudes of Blacks in the South. She presented various
examples to demonstrate her point: lynchings, slave
rebellions, resentment, dislike, boycotts by Blacks, and
the like. Smythe concluded by asserting that the nation,
in general, and the South, in particular, were faced with
the opportunity to correct this historical error and
could, in truth, produce genuine good race relations.

431. Sommer, R. and Killian, L. M.   "Areas of value difference. II. Negro-white relations." Journal of Social Psychology, 39, 1954, 237-244.

The study was done to determine differences or similarities in the ratings of a Black person by Black and White
female college students. The results showed discrepancies in the traits valued by each group. For example,
Blacks preferred the stimulus Black person to be forward,
passionate, elegant, aggressive, and persistent, while
Whites did not. Alternatively, White students preferred
the person to be witty, jovial, and shrewd, while Blacks
did not.

432. Stephenson, C. M.   "The relation between the attitudes
toward Negroes of seniors in a school of education and their
major subject." Journal of Education Research, 49, 1955,
113-121.

The purpose of the study was to determine the relationship between the attitudes of seniors in a school of
education toward Blacks and major subjects. University
seniors' mean scores on the Hinckley Scale were analyzed.
Trends by curricula showed that Social Science, Art Education, and Mathematics Science students were the most
favorable. Physical and Health Education males, Home
Economics, Industrial Arts, and Physical Education men
were the least favorable. The following were intermediate in their attitudes: language majors, Music Education, Business Education, Health and Physical Education
females, Industrial Arts, and four-year Elementary Education. However, because of the small numbers within
each group, the differences between groups were not
large enough to be significant.

433. Strong, H. H.   "Progress in race relations." Journal
of Human Relations, 4(4), 1956, 34-42.

Strong discussed what he called the four significant
periods in the history of American race relations: (1)
1661 when the first case of slavery was declared by law,
(2) when the question concerning the status of Blacks
was settled by law in 1857 in the Dred Scot decision,
(3) the development of the separate but equal doctrine
with the Plessy versus Ferguson case, and (4) the school
segregation issue which began in the courts in 1954.
The author also discussed some of the characteristics
of those who felt that Blacks were inferior and concluded

with the assertion that there might have been a time in
the past when racial segregation could have been defended
in this country on logical grounds, but that time had
passed. And, it was the belief and hope of the writer
that the people of the South could and would become suf-
ficiently interested in this matter to introduce a plan
and program which would result in getting the opponents
to see that they were lagging behind in their thinking
and in their sentiments regarding this issue and could
no longer afford to do so.

434. Stuart, I. R. "Minorities versus minorities: Cognitive, affective, and conative components of Puerto Rican and
Negro acceptance and rejection." Journal of Social Psychology, 59(1), 1963, 93-99.

The study was an investigation of how Blacks and Puerto
Ricans responded to the covert hostility and restrictions
they encountered as low-level employees in the garment
industry, how senior workers perceived and adjusted to
the influx of newcomers, and what behaviors were considered to be appropriate toward the newcomers. Examples
from grievance records showed that the Blacks and Puerto
Ricans were felt to be devious, sly, deceitful, immoral,
combative, etc., and economic competition affected relationships.

435. Summers, G. F. and Hammonds, A. D. "Effect of racial
characteristics of investigator on self-enumerated responses
to a Negro prejudice scale." Social Forces, 44(4), 1966,
515-518.

The study examined the effects of a questionnaire administrator's race on reported racial attitudes of the University of Tennessee undergraduates. In one condition,
both administrators were White. In the other condition,
one was Black, the other was White. The results showed
that socially desirable answers to an attitude scale
concerning Blacks were reported more frequently when one
of the administrators was Black. However, this finding
was more prevalent among a certain type of student than
among others, suggesting that the results be looked at
in terms of the effects of the administrator's race and
these characteristics of the respondent.

436. Thayer, S. "Lend me your ears: Racial and sexual factors in helping the deaf." Journal of Personality and Social
Psychology, 28(1), 1973(Oct), 8-11.

Thayer conducted a field experiment in Grand Central Sta-
tion in New York City in order to examine the effects of
sex and race on helping dependent deaf people. Some of
the results showed that when males helped people of their
own race, sex was a critical factor so that females were
helped more than males. When males helped other males,
White males helped the Black male more than the White

male. And Black females helped the Black female more
than the White female.

437. Thomas, A. and Sillen, S. Racism and Psychiatry. New
York: Brunner/Mazel, Publishers, 1972, 176p.

The book by Thomas and Sillen presented a discussion of
the many fallacious signs and effects of racism associated with society at large and with the psychiatric community in particular. The book was divided into such
chapters as Myths from the Past, The Genetic Fallacy,
The Sexual Mystique, The Black Patient: Separate and
Unequal, and Challenge to the Profession, among others.

438. Thune, J. M. "Racial attitudes of older adults."
Gerontologist, 7(3, Pt. 1), 1967, 179-182.

The basic aim of the research was to determine if the
racial attitudes of Black and White older adults in the
South were changing as a function of current social
change and whether attitude change could be facilitated
in these individuals under certain favoring conditions.
The article contained data which were the completion of
the first year of a three-part study. Data were obtained
from a number of tests given to four groups of males and
females who were members or would join Senior Citizens,
Incorporation Day Centers and whose average age was 68.
Four control groups were also included. Some results
showed that the White subjects were more prejudiced
(according to a social distance scale) than were the
Black subjects. In comparing the values Black subjects
felt important to themselves, to other Blacks, and to
Whites, it was found that they assigned personal values
as being most important to themselves and felt that materialistic values were most important to other Blacks.
Concerning Whites, they assigned such things as deferred
goals or long-range security, immediate goals, and personal values.

439. Tolson, H. "Counseling the 'disadvantaged.'" Personnel and Guidance Journal, 50(9), 1972(May), 735-738.

The writer looked at some of the obstacles to a sharing
relationship with clients which counselors set up by
stereotyping people and seeking to enhance their own
status. He also discussed the subtleties of racial and
economic prejudice among well-meaning, middle-class
counselors and caseworkers. (Introduction summary.)

440. Trager, H. C. and Yarrow, M. R. They Learn What They
Live: Prejudice in Young Children. New York: Harper,
1952, 392p.

Kindergarten and elementary school teachers in Philadelphia worked on a project on prejudice. They found
that children learn early cultural antagonisms although

many teachers believe children are immune to prejudice. They also found that few parents realized their responsibility for teaching democratic attitudes. An experiment designed to change attitudes showed that the children learned attitudes which were consistent with the experimental social atmosphere they experienced. It was concluded that in order to be effective in teaching democracy to children, teachers need to work in groups and have group support. (Summary of journal abstract.)

441. Tumin, M. M. "Exposure to mass media and readiness for desegregation." Public Opinion Quarterly, 21, 1957, 237-251.

White males in Guilford County, North Carolina, were interviewed in order to determine their exposure to the mass media and to obtain measures of their attitudes toward desegregation. It was found that high exposure to the mass media was associated with a low pro-segregationist sentiment on all attitude scales and that segregationist feelings were stronger on the "general belief" scale than on "what to do" scales. (Summary of journal abstract.)

442. Tumin, M. M. "Imaginary versus real children: Some southern views on desegregation." School and Society, 86, 1958, 357-360.

The attitudes of White males over 18 in a southern state show that the more children in the family the less resistant the family is to desegregation. Those with no children are the most resistant to desegregation. Difference in values of high education (income), prestige persons, and the hard core of segregationists who are recruited from the lowest rungs of the socioeconomic ladder is discussed. (Summary of journal abstract.)

443. Tumin, M. M. "Readiness and resistance to desegregation: A social portrait of the hard core." Social Forces, 36, 1958, 256-263.

Tumin conducted a study in Guilford County, North Carolina, in order to discover the qualities and quantities of readiness and resistance to desegregation among a group of 18-year-old White males who were members of the work force. Rural and urban populations were proportionately represented. Interviews were conducted by graduate students from Princeton University. Questions were designed to test hypotheses concerning the relationship between readiness for desegregation and age, education, income, residence, contact with Blacks, exposure to the mass media, and educational and occupational mobility. Among the results it was found that hard-core individuals were younger than the others, were concentrated in rural areas, fewer were white-collar workers, were less susceptible to the mass media, and achieved less education.

444. Tumin, M. M. Segregation and Desegregation: A Digest of Recent Research, 1956-1959. New York: Anti-Defamation League of B'nai B'rith, 1960 (Suppl.), 32p.

This survey and digest of recent research on segregation, desegregation, and integration of Blacks and Whites supplements an earlier digest of 1957 for the years 1951-1956. Tumin abstracted professional journals, unpublished manuscripts, theses, studies, and papers delivered at professional meetings. (Summary of journal abstract.)

445. Tumin, M. M. "Status, mobility, and anomie: A study of readiness for desegregation." British Journal of Sociology, 10, 1959, 253-267.

White adults in Guilford County, North Carolina, were interviewed in order to determine differences in readiness and resistance to desegregation. It was found that the higher the status, the lower the anomie; and the lower the anomie, the higher the readiness for desegregation. Additionally, in contrast to previous research, mobility was found to be less influential than status. (Summary of journal abstract.)

446. Tumin, M. M., Barton, P., and Burrus, P. "Education, prejudice, and discrimination: A study in readiness for desegregation." American Sociological Review, 23, 1958, 41-49.

Tumin et al. examined the major variables associated with different degrees of readiness for and resistance to desegregation among White adult males in North Carolina. Interviews were given to each subject concerning his image of Blacks, social relationships he would like to have with Blacks, sentiments he feels he would have in hypothetical contacts with Blacks, actions he would take in response to these contacts, and actions he would take in response to the question of desegregating public schools. The results generally suggested that education did not seem to reduce resistance to desegregation. However, there were distinctions between the groups in terms of their reactions to various aspects of the interview scale.

447. Van den Berghe, P. L. "The dynamics of racial prejudice: An ideal-type dichotomy." Social Forces, 37, 1958, 138-144.

Van den Berghe proposed two ideal types of racially prejudiced individuals--the paternalistic and the competitive types. The characteristics of each are cited and discussed. (Summary of journal abstract.)

448. Vander Zanden, J. W. "Desegregation: The future?" The South Atlantic Quarterly, 60(2), 1961(Spr), 205-216.

Vander Zanden discussed the attempt made by the South
to retain an independent sovereignty on the issue of
segregation. However, as he pointed out, there were
certain factors which were undermining this sovereignty.
For example, one factor discussed was the new political
orientation of states which were previously considered
southern, but were now calling themselves midwestern.
A second factor was the fact that no major political
party could concede to southern demands without seri-
ously endangering its popularity outside of the South.
And a third factor was industrialization and urbanization. Vander Zanden concluded that while the old social
order will be eroded, the new social order will not be
the idealized stated dreamed of by Blacks, it will fall
somewhere in between.

449. Vander Zanden, J. W. "Voting on segregationist refer-
enda." The Public Opinion Quarterly, 25, 1961, 92-105.

The purpose of the study was to determine whether an
inverse relationship existed between affirmative voting
on segregation and certain socioeconomic levels among
Whites in southern communities. It had been expected
that those from a higher socioeconomic level would have
more positive attitudes toward Blacks and would show
this in their voting behavior. However, the results
showed inconsistent and contradictory findings from the
15 communities studied.

450. Vanneman, R. D. and Pettigrew, T. F. "Race and relative deprivation in the urban United States." Race, 13(4),
1972, 461-486.

The study developed out of two separate literatures
within social psychology. One is concerned with the
subjective aspects of social stratification and the
other with the correlates of racial attitudes. Vanneman and Pettigrew sketched the literatures briefly
and presented their own research findings relevant
to both. (Summary of article introduction.)

451. Vedulich, R. N. and Krevanick, F. W. "Racial attitudes
and emotional response to visual representations of the
Negro." Journal of Social Psychology, 68(1), 1966, 85-93.

The study investigated physiological-emotional concomitants of racial attitudes. The authors found that the
subject's sex and the direction of extreme attitudes
were related to the amount of galvanic skin responsive-
ness to pictures of Blacks or Whites or pictures without human content. Highly prejudiced subjects and
males, in general, showed significant galvanic skin
responses to Black stimuli. (Summary of author
abstract.)

452. Venacke, W. E. "Explorations in the dynamic processes of stereotyping." Journal of Social Psychology, 43, 1956, 105-132.

The study analyzed the processes used in inter-group stereotyping. The process involved self-characteriza- tions as well as characterizations of other groups. Additionally, the stereotype terms were rated with regard to favorableness or unfavorableness. The sub- jects were Japanese, Chinese, Haoles (White), Koreans, Filipinos, Chinese-Hawaiians, and White-Hawaiians. The individuals characterized were Chinese, Japanese, Haoles, Korean, Filipino, Samoan, Hawaiian, and Black. Some of the findings were that a higher proportion of traits considered to be typical of the self were more favorable than those considered to be typical of others, but not the self. Neutral and bad groups were assigned fewer favorable traits than were good groups.

453. Vontress, C. E. "Racial differences: Impediments to rapport." Journal of Counseling Psychology, 18(1), 1971 (Jan), 7-13.

Vontress noted that American society is experiencing shifts in racial attitudes. Whites are much more hos- tile toward Blacks, and the latter are reciprocating. These effects spill over into a number of areas in which Black-White relations are involved. Rapport is diffi- cult to achieve and to maintain, especially for White counselors relating to Black clients. The difficulty in establishing counseling relationships depending upon the person's self-concept, the counselor's attitudes toward the client, the client's sex, and the region of the country from which the client comes are discussed.

454. Ward, C. D. "Attitude involvement in the absolute judgment of attitude statements." Journal of Personality and Social Psychology, 4(5), 1966, 465-476.

Ward investigated the effects of attitude, involvement, and item scale position on the judgment of attitude statements. The scale items concerned the social posi- tion of Blacks. He found that the more involved the judge was in an issue, the further from his own posi- tion was his average judgment of the statements. And, the more extreme was the judge's attitude, the closer to the other end of the continuum was his average judg- ment of the scale items.

455. Ward, C. D. "Length of attitude statements as an indi- cator of attitude." Psychological Reports, 27, 1970, 398.

Ward was concerned with examining a possible unobtrusive measure of racial attitudes. College students who scored as anti- or pro-Black were asked to write the most anti-Black statement they could think of, a neutral

statement, and the most pro-Black statement they could
imagine. Ward was interested in the length of each
statement as it might be indicative of racial attitudes.
It was found that the mean number of words used by pro-
Black students was greater for the pro statement than
for the anti statement. The means for anti-Black students were reversed, but the difference between these
two means was not significant. Additionally, pro-Black
students used more words on the pro statement than did
anti-Black students.

456. Warner, L. G. and De Fleur, M. L. "Attitude as an
interactional concept: Social constraint and social distance as intervening variables between attitudes and action."
American Sociological Review, 34(2), 1969(Apr), 153-169.

The study was concerned with gaining a better understanding of the influence of social constraint and social
distance on the relationship between attitudes and behavior. College students were subjects, and the attitude
investigated was their attitude toward Blacks. A written
attitude measure and a behavioral measure (requiring the
subject to participate in some form of action involving
Blacks) were administered. It was found that the least
prejudiced subjects were the most consistent in their
written and behavioral responses when they were not
exposed to societal sanctions which support norms that
are anti-integration. For the most prejudiced subjects,
there was a correspondence between attitudes and behavior in conditions in which their actions would be seen
since norms which were hostile to integration support
their views.

457. Watson, P. (Ed.) Psychology and Race. Chicago,
Illinois: Aldine, 1973, 491p.

The book discussed the race problem on an international
basis presenting chapters by authors from seven coun-
tries in five continents. Part one concerns aspects of
interracial interaction and contains chapters on majority and minority groups and their interactions. Part
two concerns the race variable and key issues in social
psychology. It also deals with the interaction of personality and culture, education, language, and other
issues. (Summary of journal abstract.)

458. Weigand, E. L. "Differential levels of aggression and
prejudice in selected black populations." Dissertation
Abstracts International, 31(4-B), 1970(Oct), 2269-2270.

The study measured levels of aggression in selected segments of the Black population. Black students from a
southern university as well as Black public school teachers were subjects. The experimental procedure required
the subject (paired with a Black or White confederate)
to exchange drawings they made of a house with themselves

identified on the drawing according to race, sex, age, and occupation. After the drawings were exchanged, each was to dial the amount of electric shock he thought the other individual should receive for the drawing. Subjects who had identified themselves as "Black" before the experiment were more aggressive than those who had identified themselves as "Negro" (the teachers). Those who classified themselves as Afro-Americans (college students) were the least aggressive of the subjects (their data were analyzed only in regard to the White confederate).

459. Wenckowski, C. "Black-white attitudes toward advisability of opposite race interactions." Journal of College Student Personnel, 14(4), 1973(Jul), 303-308.

Wenckowski gave a questionnaire to male and female Black and White undergraduates to assess their attitudes toward 10 types of Black-White interactions. Responses were given on a seven-point scale ranging from extremely advisable to inadvisable. It was found that Black students made significantly more extreme ratings than White students except in the case of Black and White females. White students made significantly more moderate ratings than Black students, and Blacks made significantly more uncertain ratings than Whites. The data supported the theory that those who are more involved in a certain situation choose a greater number of extreme responses. (Summary of journal abstract.)

460. Whittington, F. J. "Rebellion, religiosity, and racial prejudice." Afro-American Studies, 1(2), 1970(Oct), 139-146.

Whittington tested the degree of conformity or rebellion, along with religiosity, against degree of tolerance toward Blacks for White undergraduates. He found that students who rebelled from religious belief or from the instituional church norm of regular attendance showed less prejudice toward Blacks than those who conformed to these standards. Rebellion against religious beliefs was found to be a stronger determinant of the degree of tolerance than was religiosity and ideology. (Summary of journal abstract.)

461. Wieder, G. "Group procedures modifying attitudes of prejudice in the college classroom." Journal of Educational Psychology, 45, 1954, 332-344.

An experiment was conducted in order to compare the effectiveness of two methods of instruction in modifying prejudice. One method involved the use of group therapy procedures (non-directive and sociodrama). The second method involved a traditional lecture. It was found that the first method was the most effective. (Summary of journal abstract.)

462. Wilkerson, D. A.   "Conscious and impersonal forces in recent trends toward Negro-white school equality in Virginia."   Journal of Educational Sociology, 32, 1959(Apr), 402-408.

Wilkerson was concerned with the forces which were responsible for the progress in the direction of parity in the status of Black and White schools in the South. He discussed the "Presumed Dynamic Forces," "Recent Progress Toward Equality," and "Some Theoretical and Practical Implications."

463. Wilkinson, C. B.   "The destructiveness of myths."   In Black Psychology, R. L. Jones (Ed.).   New York: Harper & Row, Publishers, 1972.   Pp. 318-325.

Wilkinson noted that while myths were "vital ingredients of civilization (p. 319)" and could help to disclose the truth, they could also help to disguise the truth.   These assertions were made with specific reference to the destructiveness of myths which were often related to Blacks.   His work was divided into three sections concerning the Myth of the Negro Past, Sociopathological Basis for Inferiority, and The Linguists' Approach to the Pervasion of Black Related Myths.

464. Williams, J. E.   "Connotations of color names among Negroes and Caucasians."   Perceptual and Motor Skills, 18(3), 1964, 721-731.

The study explored the connotative meanings of color names to Whites and Blacks.   It was hypothesized that the color names white and black would differ in connotative meaning along the evaluative dimension of the semantic differential with white viewed as more positive than black for both races of subjects.   College students were subjects.   Two White samples, one from the North and one from the West and one Black sample from the North were tested.   Ten color names were rated on 12 scales representing the three dimensions of the semantic differential.   Analysis showed that there was no significant difference between the White groups in response to the names so their data were pooled for comparison with the Black subjects.   For the five race-related words, it was found that both groups ranked the words from white equals most good to black equals least good on the E dimension.   The words white, yellow, and red were not perceived differently by the two groups.   On the P dimension, all subjects rated yellow most weak and black most strong.   For the A dimension, brown was most passive and red was most active.

465. Williams, J. E.   "Individual differences in color name connotations as related to measures of racial attitudes." Perceptual and Motor Skills, 29, 1969, 383-386.

White college students made semantic differential ratings
of 10 color names concurrent with their participation in
four different investigations of attitudes toward Blacks.
The correlation between responses toward the color name
black on the E dimension and responses on the attitude
scales were positive. Thus, subjects who viewed the
color name more positively had somewhat more favorable
attitudes toward Blacks. Additionally, subjects who
viewed the color name brown more negatively also had
negative attitudes toward Blacks.

466. Williams, J. E., Best, D. L., Wood, I. B., and Filler,
J. W. "Changes in the connotations of racial concepts and
color names, 1963-1970." Psychological Reports, 33(3),
1973(Dec), 983-996.

Williams et al. replicated a study done in 1963 which
assessed the connotative or emotional meanings of color,
color-person, and ethnic concepts among White college
students. The purpose of the present study was to
determine whether the Black identity movement had modified the emotional meanings of these concepts. The
results showed no significant change in meanings of
the colors black and white or of the ethnic concepts
Black and White. The meanings of the color concepts
Black Person, White Person were now more related to
the ethnic concepts than to the color concepts.

467. Williams, R. L. "Black pride, academic relevance, and
individual achievement." Counseling Psychologist, 2(1),
1970, 18-22.

Williams pointed out that Blacks and Whites have different orientations to life, different psyches, and different linguistic idioms. Consequently, middle-class-
oriented measures of intelligence and achievement suit-
able for Whites are unsuitable for Blacks. Moreover,
White clinicians have not experienced Black culture,
thereby barring them from diagnosing and treating Blacks.
Blacks suffer from "niggerosis." This deals with problems like not having enough money, fighting roaches,
frozen water pipes, rats, and other symptoms of racism.
(Summary of journal abstract.)

468. Williams, W. S. "Attitudes of black and white policemen toward the opposite race." Dissertation Abstracts International, 32(1-A), 1971(Jul), 539.

Williams investigated the relationship between constructs
such as contact and attitude scores on the Attitude
Behavior Scale: Black-White/White-Negro-Law and Order
(Jordan, 1968). Three classes of variables said by
Jordan to be important determining correlates and/or
predictions of attitudes were used--demographic factors,
socio-psychological factors, and contact factors. Two
other groups were compared with the police subjects--a

predominately Black church congregation and a predominately White one. The hypothesis that Blacks would
have more positive attitudes toward Whites than Whites
had toward Blacks was not confirmed.

469. Wilner, D. M., Walkley, R. P., and Cook, W. W. "Residential proximity and intergroup relations in public housing
projects." The Journal of Social Issues, 8(1), 1952, 45-69.

The article reported two studies concerning the effects
of interracial contact between Blacks and Whites on the
racial attitudes of White females in certain housing
projects. Some of the findings indicated that women
living near Blacks had gained favorable attitudes toward
them, while those living farther away had either changed
their attitudes less or not at all. In general, the
authors noted that contact between racial groups of
equal socioeconomic status was a favorable condition
for the modification of racial attitudes.

470. Winder, A. E. "White attitudes toward Negro-white
interaction in an area of changing racial composition."
Journal of Social Psychology, 41, 1955, 85-102.

The study was done to investigate the attitudes of White
residents toward the entrance of Black householders into
the community. The hypotheses were that (a) there would
be a relationship between residential contact and White
attitudes toward participation with Blacks in a group of
interactive situations; the nature of contact in various
situations would determine whether this relationship
would result in increasing White attitudes favoring
racial prejudice or the development of healthy interracial attitudes; (b) White attitudes toward biracial
contact would vary according to the social status of
the members experiencing the contact; and (c) different
types of integrated situations would differentially be
affected by residential contact and by the social status
of the White residents. To measure White residents'
attitudes toward interactive situations with Blacks,
the experimenter presented respondents with 10 stories
describing biracial situations that might occur if
Blacks moved into the community. Results showed that
increasing biracial contact resulted in increasing
attitudes of rejection of contact and that lower status
Whites expressed a significantly greater number of
rejection attitudes than middle-class Whites.

471. Winter, S. K. "Black man's bluff." Psychology Today,
5(4), 1971(Sep), 39-43.

Three racially mixed groups of undergraduates met for
three hours a week for 10 weeks to study the groups'
functioning. In each group a Black male became the
accepted leader. They were rated as upward-negative-
backward types by the other group members using Bales'

Interpersonal Rating System. The Blacks were able to
maintain leadership roles in spite of being in the
minority, at least partially because group members
shared (but did not discuss) cultural myths concerning
Blacks and Whites. (Summary of journal abstract.)

472. Woodmansee, J. J., Jr. "An evaluation of pupil
response as a measure of attitude toward Negroes." Dissertation Abstracts, 26(11), 1966, 6896-6897.

The purpose of the study was to evaluate pupil response
in relation to attitudinally affective stimuli and to
evaluate the influence of the light reflex, the near
vision reflex, and the arousal decrement effect in pupil
constriction. Females who had different attitudes
toward Blacks looked at four Black-content pictures
while their left eye was photographed. The results
were that on the first presentation of the pictures,
the average pupil response was -.10 percent for anti-
Black subjects and +2.65 percent for equalitarian subjects. However, when the data were examined across
the eight presentations of the pictures, the groups
did not differ significantly.

473. Woofter, T. J. Southern Race Progress: The Wavering
Color Line. Washington, D.C.: Public Affairs Press, 1957,
180p.

Woofter presented an autobiographical-sociological
analysis of southern race relations describing progress
and regress from Reconstruction to the Supreme Court
decision on school segregation. He also described the
effects of the Phelps-Stokes Fund, Commission on Interracial Cooperation on the racial problem in the South.
Through anecdote, he analyzed various aspects of the
race problem. (Summary of journal abstract.)

474. Word, C. O., Zanna, M. P., and Cooper, J. "The non-
verbal mediation of self-fulfilling prophecies in interracial interaction." Journal of Experimental Social Psychology, 10(2), 1974, 109-120.

Two experiments were designed to demonstrate the existence of a self-fulfilling prophecy mediated by non-
verbal behavior in an interracial interaction. The
results of Experiment I which used naive White job
interviewers and trained White and Black job applicants
demonstrated that Black applicants received less imme-
diacy, higher rates of speech errors, and shorter
amounts of interview time. Experiment II used naive
White applicants and trained White interviewers. In
this experiment, subject applicants received behavior
that approximated that given either the Black or White
applicants in Experiment I. The main results indicated
that subjects treated like the Blacks of Experiment I
were judged to perform less adequately and to be more

nervous in the interview situation than subjects treated
like the Whites of that experiment. The former subjects
also reciprocated with less proximate positions and rated
the interviewers as being less adequate and friendly.
All of this behavior was recorded by two judges placed
behind one-way mirrors.

475. Yoshino, R. I. "The stereotype of the Negro and his
high-priced car." Sociology and Social Research, 44, 1959,
112-118.

Yoshino conducted a study to determine whether the observation that Blacks tend to own Cadillacs was a stereotype and whether there was any association between the
type of car owned and the social class to which the Black
person belonged. An open-ended interview and survey were
made within a Black, conservative, middle-class neighborhood. It was found that of the 93 families interviewed, only three owned Cadillacs. Furthermore, there
was no significant association between make of car and
social class.

AUTHOR INDEX

The numbers after each name refer to
item numbers in the bibliography.

SUBJECT INDEX

The numbers after each name refer to
item numbers in the bibliography.

A

academic achievement, 62
achievement orientation, 115
adolescents, 24, 113
Afro-American, 40
Africans, 369
age, 21, 33, 34, 42, 43, 54,
76, 189, 244, 308, 342, 362
aggression, 10, 279, 458
Alabama, 227
alienation, 100
American Blacks, 265, 274
American-Chinese, 64
American Indians, 196, 327
Americans, 195, 249
anomie, 195, 445
anti-Black, 213, 455
anti-Black attitudes, 136,
188
anti-Black prejudice, 2, 161,
241
anti-Black subjects, 174, 472
anti-Semitism, 188
anti-White attitudes, 105
anti-White ideologies, 203
anti-White prejudice, 2
anxiety, 3, 78, 97
Arizona State University, 382
Assertion Training, 180
Atlanta, 370
attitude change, 4, 7, 17,
18, 32, 148, 149, 150, 373
attitudes, 4, 13, 15, 17, 18,
20, 25, 27, 28, 31, 32, 46,
48, 51, 58, 61, 62, 66,
134, 196, 197, 209, 297,
363
attitudes toward Blacks, 135,
137, 242, 244, 247, 284,
324, 325, 382, 385, 415, 465

attitudes toward minorities,
411
Attitudes Toward Minority
Group Scale, 196
attitudes toward race, 119
attitudes toward race relations, 355
authoritarianism, 55, 71, 74,
179, 195, 203

B

Bales' Interpersonal Rating
System, 471
Baptist religion, 168
beliefs, 55, 166, 182, 210,
296, 304
bill of rights, 196, 411
Birmingham, 370
Bogardus Social Distance
Scale, 398, 417
Boston, 263
boys, 10, 33, 35, 43, 47, 56,
57, 76
Black, 37, 41, 42, 52, 53,
55, 56, 57, 61, 63, 107,
109, 157, 451
Black Americans, 414
Black art, 11
Black authors, 102
Black boys, 35, 103
Black children, 8, 16, 19,
26, 34, 37, 39, 40, 54, 60,
61, 64, 69, 72, 73, 75, 80,
87, 88, 92, 93, 98, 109,
110, 119, 121, 223, 346
Black child's, 19
Black college students, 36,
165, 166, 185, 233, 273,
274

173

Hawaiian, 452
Head-Start, 23
health, 362
high school students, 20
hostility, 24
housing discrimination, 292
human relations, 25

I

identification, 54, 64, 72
Indian, 108, 217, 376
individuation, 26
informal racial contact, 97
in-group, 4, 279
integrated, 18, 51, 57
integrated children, 62
integrated classrooms, 19,
   101
integrated housing project,
   147
integrated school, 2, 46, 51,
   66, 133, 134
integration, 3, 19, 25, 38,
   57, 62, 71, 89, 90, 164,
   268, 309, 327, 328, 329,
   346, 355, 373, 385, 398
intelligence, 121
IQ scores, 1
internal locus of control,
   182
interracial behaviors, 30
interracial contact, 27, 80,
   101, 106, 128, 236, 469
interracial friendships, 2
interracial group, 367
interracial marriage, 96
interracial situations, 85
intolerance, 65
Irish, 217
isolation, 100
Italian-Americans, 393
Italians, 217

J

Japanese, 65, 217, 261, 374,
   376, 408, 452
Japanese-Americans, 196, 375,
   393
Jewish, 217, 265
Jewish-Americans, 76, 414
Jewish children, 223
Jews, 65, 70, 78, 160, 194,
   196, 223, 285, 302, 327,
   376, 393

K

Kalamazoo, Michigan, 328
kindergarten children, 12,
   16
Korea, 379
Koreans, 452
Korean War, 384

L

Ladies Home Journal, 424
lazy, 65
Level of Aspiration measure,
   59
level of education, 18
level of prejudice, 205
liberal, 284, 308
liberal attitudes, 197
Life, 424
light-skinned Blacks, 114,
   157, 405
light-skinned subjects, 49
Likert-type Negro Attitude
   Test, 139
Likert-type scale, 196, 385
Lithuanian-American, 191
Little Rock, Arkansas, 246
Los Angeles, 333, 405
lower-class Blacks, 10, 156
lower-class boys, 92
lower-class girls, 92
lower-class Whites, 156
lower-middle-class junior
   high school students, 94

M

majority members, 7
male experimenters, 34
manifest anxiety, 3
marital status, 189
Marlow-Crowne Social Desirability Scale, 236
medium-dark Black, 95
Mexican-American, 108, 111,
   334, 393,
Mexicans, 65, 327, 376, 408
middle-class backgrounds, 40
middle-class Black, 10, 173,
   262
middle-class children, 34
Midwest, 338
Minneapolis, 223, 413
minorities, 13, 182, 302,
   326

ABOUT THE AUTHOR

Constance E. Obudho (Ph.D. candidate at Rutgers University in psychology with special emphasis in Social/Personality Psychology) is a Predoctoral Fellow at the Institute for Research in Human Development, Educational Testing Service, Princeton, New Jersey. She was formerly a Teaching Assistant in the Department of Psychology, Livingston College, Rutgers University from 1972 to 1975. She is currently a member of the Society for the Psychological Study of Social Issues and the Rutgers University College Honor Society. Her areas of interest include nonverbal communication and racial attitudes.

Her publications include the following: *Urbanization, City and Regional Planning in Metropolitan Kisumu, Kenya: Bibliographical Survey of an East African City* co-authored with R. A. Obudho (Monticello, Illinois: Council of Planning Librarians, Exchange Bibliography, No. 278, April, 1972); "Clean is beautiful: The effects of race and cleanliness on racial preferences" with Yakov M. Epstein and Edward Krupat, *Journal of Social Issues*, 1975, also in *Readings and Conversation in Social Psychology: Psychology is Social* by Edward Krupat (Oakland, New Jersey: Scott, Foresman & Company, 1975; and *The Proxemic Behavior of Man and Animals: Annotated Bibliography* (Monticello, Illinois: Council of Planning Librarians Exchange Bibliography No. 646 and 647, September, 1974).